Hume's Philosophy of Religion

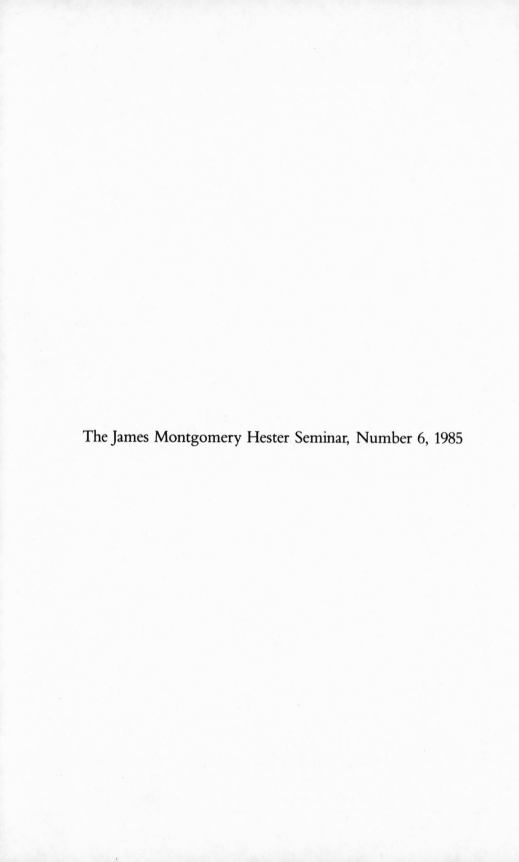

The James Montgomery Hester Seminar, Number 6, 1985

Hume's
Philosophy of Religion

The Sixth James Montgomery Hester Seminar

Lectures by
Antony Flew
Donald Livingston
George I. Mavrodes
David Fate Norton

Wake Forest University Press
Winston-Salem, North Carolina

© 1986 Wake Forest University
Department of Philosophy
Winston-Salem, North Carolina 27109
All rights reserved.
Printed in the United States of America

Produced by Book Service Associates
Winston-Salem, N.C. 27108-0830 • SAN 294-9059
ISSN 0891-1894

Contents

Notes on the Contributors

Trained in Oxford during the heyday of Gilbert Ryle and John Austin, Antony Flew has held full-time teaching positions in Oxford, Aberdeen, Keele, and Reading as well as visiting appointments in the United States, Canada, Australia, and Malawi. The twenty-two books for which he has been wholly or partly responsible (as author or editor, coauthor or coeditor) include: *Logic and Language* (First and Second Series); *New Essays in Philosophical Theology; Hume's Philosophy of Belief; God and Philosphy* (reissued as *God: A Critical Enquiry*); *The Presumption of Atheism* (reissued as *God, Freedom and Immortality*); *A Rational Animal; The Politics of Procrustes;* and *Darwinian Evolution.*

Donald Livingston is associate professor of philosophy at Emory University. He was educated at Wake Forest University and Washington University. He taught at Northern Illinois University from 1967 to 1983 and was a National Endowment for the Humanities independent study fellow in 1978-79. He specializes in Hume, the Scottish Enlightenment, and philosophy of history. He is coeditor of *Hume: A Re-Evaluation,* the author of many articles on Hume, and *Hume's Philosophy of Common Life,* published in 1984 by the University of Chicago Press.

George Ion Mavrodes was educated at Oregon State College, Western Baptist Seminary, and the University of Michigan. He taught at Princeton University in 1961-62 and rose from assistant to full professor at the University of Michigan during the years 1962-73. He is the author of *Belief in God: A Study in the Epistemology of Religion* and of many scholarly articles, including: "Conventions and the Morality of War," "The Life Everlasting and the Bodily Criterion of Identity," "Real vs. Deceptive Mystical Experiences," and "The Morality of Selling Human Organs."

David Fate Norton is professor of philosophy at McGill University. He did his graduate work at the University of California, San Diego, where he has also taught. He specializes in 18th-century British, especially Scottish, philosophy (Hutcheson, Hume, and Reid). He is also editor of the *Journal of the History of Philosophy* and coeditor of *McGill Hume Studies.* His recent publications include *David Hume, Common-Sense Moralist, Sceptical Metaphysician.*

Foreword

I am grateful to Professor Marcus Hester for his invitation to write a brief prefatory note to this volume. It provides me an opportunity to thank him and other members of the Department of Philosophy at Wake Forest for their efforts in bringing this series of the James Montgomery Hester Seminar to the campus and now into print. This series is a living memorial to our gratitude to James Montgomery Hester, whose benefaction has made this program possible.

I have a very different debt of gratitude to discharge to this subject and to these scholars. In the early 1960s I wrote a doctoral dissertation on the moral philosophy of David Hume. That project brought me into active contact across the years with these men and these themes. To have these distinguished scholars at Wake Forest was for me an intellectual homecoming of the most welcome sort.

David Norton edited (and improved) one of the first articles I published regarding Hume. Don Livingston, one of our own alumni, was a founder of the David Hume Society. I was fortunate to have been present and on the program at its charter session. George Mavrodes and Antony Flew wrote books and articles which I studied to my great profit. I was fortunate to be in their company on occasions which brought both intellectual and personal pleasure.

The history of philosophy is an ever changing discipline. Each era must ask new and revised questions of the "old masters" of philosophy. David Hume's work has had a remarkable impact on recent philosophical thought. This volume is both a contribution and a tribute to the continuing importance and vitality of this greatest of the empiricists.

Thomas K. Hearn, Jr.
Professor of Philosophy and President
Wake Forest University

Antony Flew

The Impossibility

Of the Miraculous

Some misunderstandings of and about the first *Enquiry*, misunderstandings which were widespread twenty-five years ago when I was writing *Hume's Philosophy of Belief*,[1] are now, if not altogether extinct, at any rate much less common. For instance: when Peter Nidditch produced his Third Edition of the Clarendon text it was "for various practical reasons" apparently impossible to excise, or even to revise or annotate, the original Editor's Introduction of 1893.[2] Nevertheless, if only perhaps because introductions are so rarely read, no one in recent years seems to have accepted Selby-Bigge's confident contentions: that Sections X and XI "do not add anything" to the "general speculative position" presented in this *Enquiry;* or that "their insertion," like that of Part II of Section VIII, "may be ascribed to Hume's ambition to disturb the zealots at all costs."[3]

Again, in appreciating that these sections, and indeed that part too, are centrally relevant to his Lockean project, critics are almost bound also to discover what it was that Hume was arguing against. Certainly he makes it very clear from the beginning, in Section I, not only what the project was but also that his intentions in carrying it out were militantly secularizing. The Lockean inspiration was underlined when in the collected edition of 1758 he gave the book its present title; the secularizing intentions needed no further underlining. The project "is to enquire seriously into the nature of human understanding, and show, from an exact analysis of its powers and capacity, that it is by no means fitted" for certain "remote and abstract subjects." And what are these? They are the subjects or pseudo subjects of "a considerable part of metaphysics," which is "not properly a science." They "arise either from the fruitless efforts of human vanity . . . or from the craft of popular superstitions. . . . Chaced from the open country, these robbers fly into the forest, and lie in wait to break in upon every unguarded avenue of the mind, and overwhelm it with religious fears and prejudices."[4]

The prime source for finding what Sections X and XI are together arguing against is Leslie Stephen's classic *English Thought in the Eighteenth Century*.[5] What Hume wants to demolish, and what he has to demolish if the task which he has set himself is to be accomplished, is a programme for a systematic and rational Christian apologetic. This consisted of two stages. The first, while appealing only to natural reason and common experience, laboured to establish the existence and certain minimal characteristics of God. The second tried to supplement this inevitably somewhat sketchy religion of nature with a more abundant Revelation.

The general validity of such a programme, although not that of any particular positive proof of Natural Theology, was defined as dogma necessary to salvation by what it is now proper to call the First Vatican Council of 1870-71. (However, we should perhaps notice in passing that, since the Second Vatican Council touched off the progressive Protestantization of the Roman Church, this defined dogma appears to have become one of the items rather rarely picked by those professing Catholics who insist on choosing out of the historic deposit of the Faith their own individual anthologies of credibility.) The relevant canon dealing with the second stage neither hesitates nor compromises: "If anyone shall say . . . that miracles can never be known for certain, or that the divine origin of the Christian religion cannot properly be proved by them: let them be anathema."[6]

The fact that Section X is one half of Hume's response to the challenge of the traditional systematic rational apologetic for Christianity does seem to be widely understood nowadays. If the issues arising are not very much or very vigorously discussed, then this neglect is to be explained by reference not to ignorance of the historical context but rather to a lack of interest in either the erection or, consequently, the demolition of such structures. Yet there was a time when it was usual to talk both as if Hume had published "Of Miracles" as a separate essay, and in complete unawareness of the fact that his "everlasting check" was only one move in a more comprehensive game. This is true, for instance, of A. E. Taylor's "David Hume and the Miraculous."[7] It is matter for wry and salutary contemplation that this ill-starred study was first delivered as a Sir Leslie Stephen lecture, beginning with a seemly tribute to Stephen's writings on eighteenth-century thought. For there can be few of us who cannot feel the weight of beams in our own eyes when someone quotes the saying: "The classics are like the nobility; we learn their titles and thereafter claim acquaintance with them."

We can, therefore, take it as today generally understood: both that Sections X and XI are integral to the whole project of the first *Enquiry;* and that Hume's main concern in both is to undermine the established rational apologetic. It also appears to be generally recognized that "Of Miracles" is about evidence rather than about fact. Thus, at least in the first instance, the question is not whether miracles actually have occurred and do occur but whether and, if so, how anyone could know that this was so. Hume's special concern is, of course, with the more particular question "whether a miracle can ever be so proved, so as to be the foundation of a system of religion."[8] This is, presumably, some part of the reason so many people miss the point that Section X is a contribution not only to the philosophy of religion but also to the philosophy of history.

It is, as I noted in *Hume's Philosophy of Belief,* most remarkable that neither F. H. Bradley in *The Presuppositions of Critical History* nor R. G. Collingwood in *The Idea of History* makes any mention at all of Hume's treatment "Of Miracles."[9] But even more recent introductions to the philosophy of history do scant justice to it. W. H. Walsh refers to "the classical discussions of historical testimony to be found in Hume's Essay of Miracles . . . and Bradley's *Presuppositions of Critical History";* adding that "Hume says, in effect, that we cannot give credence to accounts of events in the past the occurrence of which would have abrogated the laws of physical nature; Bradley . . . says we can believe about the past only that which bears some analogy to what we have known in our own experience."[10] But elsewhere, after observing that "As Hume saw, we do distinguish in the sphere of matter of fact between what we consider to be 'proved' and what we regard as merely 'probable'," Walsh has nothing to say about what is supposed to be factually or practically as opposed to "logically possible."[11]

In what is in total a rather richer book, R. F. Atkinson refers frequently to Hume, yet never to this Section X.[12] It is significant that in discussing questions about laws of nature in history Atkinson takes no account of the contention that such laws necessarily carry implications of practical as opposed to logical necessity, of practical as opposed to logical impossibility.[13] In the later chapter on "Causation" we do hear about "fundamental causes, which may be said to render the event inevitable," and about other causes bringing about or preventing various outcomes.[14] Much too is soundly said about the difficulties of squaring "the so-called 'regularity' theory of causation, which derives from Hume's *Treatise*," with one-off causal judgements of the kind so commonly and so confidently made both by historians and by laypersons.[15] But in the end Atkinson is no readier than Walsh to accept, and to bring out the consequences of accepting, that the concept of cause as well the concept of law of nature essentially includes notions of both practical necessity and practical impossibility.[16]

The main purpose of the present paper is to urge such acceptance in the context of the discussion of Section X of the first *Enquiry*, and to display the consequences in that context. Although our brief here at Wake Forest is to consider only the philosophy of religion, these consequences cannot but have some bearing on the philosophy of history also.

Starting now to execute this main purpose we need first to recall once more Hume's insistence that for him the chief question was "whether a miracle can [ever] be proved so as to be the foundation of a system of religion." So what is the reason an answer to this question is so important, and so indispensable to the whole project of this first *Enquiry?*

In a nutshell, it is that there would seem to be no other way of showing that the Christian system, or indeed any other and rival candidate, is a genuine Revelation of the true God. To serve as the key term in such a demonstration the word "miracle" has to be construed, as both Hume himself and all his contemporary opponents did construe it, in a very strong sense. It must, that is, involve an overriding of a law of nature; a doing of what is known to be naturally impossible by a Power which is, by this very overriding, shown to be Supernatural and Supreme.

Only if this is given can the occurrence of a miracle under the auspices of some particular system of belief constitute an inexpugnable Divine endorsement of that system. Without appreciating the rationality and the straightforwardness of this approach to the settling of disputes between the protagonists of incompatible sets of religious beliefs, we cannot hope to understand: either Hume's insistence that the miracle stories of rival religions must be assessed as not merely different but contrary,[18] or the delighted attention which he gives to the then recent Affair of the Abbé Paris.[19] It was precisely and only because both the Jansenists and the Jesuits did accept these principles that both parties were so keen to show, the one that miracles had occurred at that cleric's tomb, and the other that they had not.

. There are many today who, while continuing to claim the Christian name, feel forced to abandon that strong conception of the miraculous, and indeed the whole rational apologetic for which it provides a crucial term. This puts them in a doubly desperate position. In the first place, they can scarcely hope to develop—what too often they do not even bother to seek—any better alternative way of trying to show that their faith is reasonable.

In the second place, one particular miracle story—that of what myriads of old-fashioned Easter sermons have insisted must be the miracle of miracles—is not merely evidence for the authenticity of the Christian Revelation but also integral to it. It is, that is to say, the very heart and essence of the Gospel message: that the second person of the Trinity became man; that He was born of woman, if not necessarily of a virgin; that He preached the word of his Father in the Galilee; that He was crucified, dead and buried; *and that He rose again on the third day.* There is no doubt some room for disagreement among Christians about the precise nature of that miracle of miracles. But against any defection from its truly miraculous character the objection of St. Paul must be, surely, quite decisive? "And if

Christ be not risen, then is our preaching vain, your faith is also vain."[20] It was not, therefore, any wanton desire to shock which led Hume to introduce his factitious legend of the Resurrection of Elizabeth the Great.[21] It was, rather, the need to press his argument home.

If we bear in mind what Hume has been saying in earlier sections of the first *Enquiry,* then we should expect that argument to be quite other than it is. Thus in Section VIII he draws upon the findings of Sections IV, V and VII to sustain a compatibilism "Of Liberty and Necessity." Given what he is pleased to call "a just and precise idea of *necessity*"—which in truth involves only regularity and no sort of necessity at all— then "this reconciling project" can scarcely fail to go through at the trot.[22] Given again that same denatured Humean notion of practical necessity we should expect Hume to have contended that there must be something conceptually vicious about the very suggestion "Of Miracles." Had he been able to make good on such a contention he would have succeeded in exploding the second stage of the standard rational apologetic for Christianity; as well as demolishing what is, arguably, one of the essential concepts of that "system of religion."

The fact that scarcely anyone ever has expected what should have been expected can be put down as in part a consequence of failure to read Section X in the context of the first *Enquiry* as a whole. It was perhaps in an attempt to remedy this failure that Hume eventually gave the book its present title. But a much more important part of the explanation has to be found in Hume's own failure, and the consequent failure of successive generations of Humeans, to recognize that notions of practical necessity and of practical impossibility are essentially involved in the idea of laws of nature and that these notions are much stronger than that of even the most perfect regularity. Tacitly and, it would seem, all unwittingly, Hume himself in effect admits this: not only at the beginning of Part I and throughout

Part II of Section VIII[23] but also, and most strikingly, in Part I of Section X.

For he writes there: "But in order to encrease the probability against the testimony of witnesses, let us suppose that the fact, which they affirm, instead of being only marvellous, is really miraculous." The following paragraph begins: "A miracle is a violation of the laws of nature; and, as a firm and unalterable experience has established these laws, the proof against a miracle, from the very nature of the fact, is as entire as any argument from experience can possibly be imagined."[24]

This is, I submit, one of the most powerful, profound and important of all Hume's philosophical arguments. It is, nevertheless, one which he himself is entitled to employ only *ad hominem*. For the reason the establishment of a law of nature constitutes a "proof against a miracle . . . as entire as any argument from experience can possible be imagined" is that a violation of a true law of nature must be, by definition, physically (and naturally) impossible; just as obedience to such true laws of nature is, correspondingly, physically (and naturally) necessary. Indeed, unless conceptual room is thus parenthetically made for the logical possibility of supernatural overridings, as in truth it always was made both by Hume and by his contemporary opponents, such a violation must be a logical impossibility also.

But Hume's own discrediting account of physical necessity, and consequently of physical impossibility also, leaves him with no way of opening up a suitably wide gulf between "being only marvellous" and being "really miraculous."[25] Nor can Hume consistently allow that "any argument from experience" constitutes any sort of proof of either physical necessity or physical impossibility. That avenue is open only to those able and willing to defend the claims that we do all of us in making and in failing to make things happen have experience of both the one and the other,[26] and that it is thus and only thus that we are able to acquire these two fundamental concepts.[27]

We who are ever ready to allow to "the good David" the benefit of every doubt will want here to give a fair run to the suggestion that the argument of Section X is, and properly, exclusively *ad hominem*. Certainly he does begin by suggesting that he is recommending a purely defensive posture: "Nothing is so convenient as a decisive argument of this kind, which must at least *silence* the most arrogant bigotry and superstition, and free us from their impertinent solicitations." Those then who should find this proposed "everlasting check" invaluable are persons of sense rather than of faith: "A wise man," Hume goes on to insist, "proportions his belief to the evidence."[28]

So far, yet only so far, so good. For the unfortunate truth is that, both here and later, Hume's own dismissals of all stories of the miraculous are themselves grounded upon precisely that "most powerful, profound and important" argument quoted in the last paragraph but one: "A miracle is a violation of the laws of nature; and as a firm and unalterable experience has established these laws, the proof against a miracle, from the very nature of the fact, is as entire as any argument from experience can possibly be imagined."

That Hume did not see the implications for this argument of some of his other most characteristic contentions becomes the less surprising to the extent that we familiarize ourselves with similar failures on the part of our own contemporaries. For, whether or not they actually have benefitted, these contemporaries have had the opportunity of benefitting from subsequent criticism. For instance: *The Times* of London recently printed a letter signed by the president of the Linnaean Society and a string of other leading scientists. One paragraph read: "It is not logically valid to use science as an argument against miracles. To believe that miracles cannot happen is as much an act of faith as to believe that they can happen."[29]

To this letter the editor of *Modern Geology* responded by conceding the claim of those first correspondents, and retreating to what he hoped would be stronger ground: "Your correspondents correctly insist that it is not logically valid to use science as an argument against miracles. To believe that miracles cannot happen is indeed an act of faith. But that surely is not the issue. The question is not whether they can, but have they ever."

Both parties to this correspondence were thus hopelessly and fundamentally in error. For unless there are, and can be known to be, laws of nature entailing that the occurrence of certain sorts of events would be physically (and naturally) impossible while that of other sorts is physically (and naturally) necessary, then it must be absurd even to suggest that there might be, and that we might know that there have been, some supernatural overridings of such laws!

Once these fundamentals have been established, and no sooner, we can proceed to put the evidential Humean variant of the alternative question proposed by the editor of *Modern Geology:* Could we ever know that a miracle had occurred? It is in response to this question that Hume goes on to argue, in the two final paragraphs of Part I, that there cannot but be a conflict, even a contradiction, within any suitably comprehensive case for saying that a miracle has actually occurred. Such a case has to show first, that the supposed laws, of which the actual occurrence of the putatively miraculous events would constitute an overriding, do in fact obtain, and second, that the overridings have actually occurred.

All evidence for the first proposition, however, is at the same time evidence against the second; and the other way about. For to say that a law of nature obtains, just is to say that it is (not logically or a priori but naturally and practically) impossible for any events to occur such that these events would by their occurring falsify the universal and nomological (law-stating) proposition which expresses that law of nature. Thus to show that a law of nature obtains, just is to show that the occurrence of exceptions is naturally impossible; while to show that even one "exception" has occurred would be to show that that law, at least in that formulation, did not obtain.

This conflict, a contradiction, can of course be resolved; but only at what must here be an unacceptable price. Certainly it is open to spokespersons for the miraculous to claim that their alleged revelations provide them with the necessary criteria. These are the criteria which they need for distinguishing between, on the one hand, those exceptions which as overridings by a Power above and outside Nature do not constitute true falsifications of the supposed laws of nature and, on the other hand, those "exceptions" which are truly falsifying—and hence call for further and hopefully more successful creative work by our scientists.

It is, or ought to be, obvious why such a resolution cannot be accepted by anyone committed to the traditional apologetic. If the occurrence of a miracle is to serve as an endorsement of a candidate revelation, then we have to excogitate some means entirely independent of that putative revelation by which this guarantee itself can be recognized. A parallel objection arises if, with what has become a fashionable school in theology, you urge that miracles are not really overridings but signs. If a sign is to signify to the unbeliever, then there has to be some means independent of the doctrinal system itself whereby the signs may be identified as such and their significations understood.

Hume's presentation in Part I of Section X has two weaknesses.

About the first and more important of these much has been said already. It is that he takes no account of the upsetting implications of his own earlier and most cherished contentions. According to him laws of nature, insofar as they are descriptive of the phenomena to which they apply, state only that ongoings of one particular sort will in fact always be accompanied by ongoings of another particular sort. They do not state, neither do they imply, that, once an event of the one sort has occurred, it must be impossible by any human or other natural force to prevent the occurrence of an event of the other sort. Laws of nature, therefore, as thus understood by Hume, or rather misunderstood, could provide no purchase for any dramatically overriding manifestations of the definitionally Supernatural Deity.

Again, Humean causes are only followed by, they do not bring about, their effects: the occurrence of the cause event, that is, does not either make necessary the occurrence of the effect event or make impossible its nonoccurrence. The only necessity involved, according to Hume, is a muddled notion in us as we think about causes. It is a matter of our feeling the force of habitual associations of resembling ideas and impressions and projecting this muddle out onto realities among which there are to be found no necessities of any kind.

The second, and rather uninteresting, weakness arises because Hume has not yet altogether abandoned one hope cherished at the time of the *Treatise.* This is the hope of producing a kind of mechanics of consciousness, with principles of the association of ideas relating moments of consciousness in something like the way in which the principles of classical mechanics related the "hard, massy and impenetrable" billiard balls of atomic theory. Here the best response is to begin by appreciating what Hume was understandably, if no doubt misguidedly, trying to do, next perhaps to smile at his efforts, and finally to pass on. Take, as an example of his laughably literalistic and plonkingly quantitative interpretation of the weighing of evidence, this statement: "A hundred instances or experiments on one side, and fifty on another, afford a doubtful expectation of any event. . . . In all cases, we must balance the opposite experiments, when they are opposite, and deduct the smaller number from the greater, in order to know the exact force of the superior evidence."[30]

So far we have followed Hume in concentrating upon the question of proving a miracle "so as to be the foundation of a system of religion." But the argument expounded in Part I of Section X and applied in Part II has a far more extensive application. It is, he claims, "a decisive argument . . . which must as least *silence* the most arrogant bigotry and superstition, and free us from their impertinent solicitations . . . an argument which . . . will . . . with the wise and learned, be an everlasting check to all kinds of superstitious delusion."[31]

It is sometimes thought that there is no more to this "everlasting check" than a trite reminder that, because the occurrence of a miracle must be very improbable, it needs to be quite exceptionally well evidenced. But C. S. Peirce, who seems never to have exploited it fully, had the vital interpretative clue in his hands when he remarked: "The whole of modern 'higher criticism' of ancient history in general . . . is based upon the same logic as is used by Hume."[32] The truth is that Hume's discussion "Of Miracles", besides belonging both to the philosophy of religion and to the philosophy of history, also has a major bearing on the philosophy of science in general, and in particular, on that of the religion-related would-be science of parapsychology.

What, with some lapses and hesitations, Hume is contending is that the criteria by which we must assess historical testimony, and the general presumptions which alone allow us to interpret the detritus of the past as historical evidence, must inevitably rule out any possibility of establishing definitively, upon purely historical evidence, that some genuinely miraculous event has indeed occurred.

His fundamental theses are: first, that the detritus of the past cannot be construed as any sort of historical evidence unless we presume that the same basic regularities obtained then as obtain today; and second, that in trying as best he may to determine what actually happened, the historian has to employ as criteria all his present knowledge and presumed knowledge of what is probable or improbable, possible or impossible. In the *Treatise* Hume argued that it is only upon such presumptions that we can justify even the basic conclusion that certain kinds of ink marks on old pieces of paper constitute testimonial evidence.[33] Earlier in Part I of Section VIII of this first *Enquiry* he has urged the inescapable importance of having such criteria, while, in a footnote to Section X, he quotes with approval the reasoning of the famous physician De Sylva in the contested case of a Mademoiselle Thibaut: "It was impossible she could have been so ill as was proved by witnesses," De Sylva argued, "because it was impossible that she could, in so short a time, have recovered so perfectly as he found her."[34]

Two serious faults in Hume's presentation in Part II of Section X may obscure the force and soundness of De Sylva's reasoning, and the fact that this sort of application of canons to evidence is absolutely essential to the very possibility of critical history. The first fault is that—contrary to his own sceptical principles—Hume tends to take it for granted that whatever in his own day he and all his fellow persons of sense firmly believed about the order of nature constituted not just well-grounded yet always humanly fallible opinion but the definitive and incorrigible last word. He is thus betrayed into rejecting as downright impossible certain reported phenomena which the progress of abnormal psychology and psychosomatic medicine has since shown to have been perfectly possible.

For instance: like several other eighteenth-century sceptics Hume makes much of the supposed miracles supposedly wrought in Egypt by the soldier Emperor Vespasian, suggesting, if never perhaps outright stating, that the evidence in this case is far and away stronger than that for any of the miracle stories of the *New Testament*. Suppose now that we are so conscientiously curious as actually to refer to the accounts given in the Roman historians Suetonius and Tacitus.[35] We find that, according to Suetonius, when the Emperor was in Egypt "two labourers, one blind and the other lame, approached him, begging to be healed; apparently the god Serapis had promised them in a dream that if Vespasian would consent to spit in the blind man's eye and touch the lame man's leg with his heel, both would be cured." According to the longer account in Tacitus (in which the lame man becomes a man with a withered hand), Vespasian "asked the doctors for an opinion whether blindness and atrophy of this sort were curable by human means. The doctors were eloquent about the various possibilities: the blind man's vision was not completely destroyed, and if certain impediments were removed, his sight would return; the other man's limb had been dislocated, but could be put right by correct treatment. . . . Anyway, if a cure were effected, the credit would go to the ruler; if it failed, the poor wretches would have to bear the ridicule." Both historians go on to tell us that Vespasian did what he had been asked to do and that the two patients were in consequence cured.

So, given those medical reports insisting on the absence of any gross organic lesions, and in the light of what has since been learned about psychosomatic possibilities, we now have to say not that Vespasian did after all perform two miracles of healing during his Egyptian tour, and that this is something which we now know on sound historical grounds, but that what Hume dismissed as something which could not have occurred, because its occurence would have been miraculous, in fact did occur but was not miraculous. Our reasons for saying that the cures were indeed effected is at the same time our reason for saying that they were not miraculous.

Before moving on to the second fault let us notice another case equally Classical but much less disputed. In Herodotus— "the father of critical history"—we read that at the time of the Pharaoh Necho II (about 600 B.C.) Phoenician sailors claimed to have circumnavigated Africa.[36] They said that they had sailed South down what we call the Red Sea and arrived at the Mediterranean coast of Egypt nearly three years later. The interesting thing for us is their report that during the voyage the position of the sun shifted from the South to the North, and back again. Herodotus, recording that they said this, states that he himself does not believe what they said. He had two good reasons for disbelief: first, he knew that Phoenician and indeed other sailors are apt to tell tall tales; and second, he took it that he knew that what the sailors reported was impossible. Herodotus therefore had good reason to dismiss this story, and did in fact dismiss it.

But for us, of course, what was for Herodotus an excellent reason for incredulity is the decisive ground for believing that Phoenicians did in fact circumnavigate Africa at this time. They could scarcely have got this thing about the changing relative position of the sun right unless they had actually made the voyage which they said they had made. Both Herodotus and the successors who have on this point put him right were employing the same sound historical methods, the only methods possible for the critical historian.

Both he and we, that is, are and cannot but be committed, in interpreting and assessing the detritus of the past as historical evidence, to appealing to all that we know or think we know about what is probable or improbable, possible or impossible. Thus Herodotus, in trying to interpret the evidence of the Phoenicians, rightly appealed to what he knew, or thought he knew, about astronomy and geography. We, following exactly the same fundamental principles of historical reconstruction, but having the advantage over him of knowing more about astronomy and geography, reach different conclusions, albeit by fundamentally the same methods.

The second serious fault in Hume's presentation in Part II of Section X arises from the inadequacies of his accounts of causation and of laws of nature. For, as must have become obvious from previous discussion of those inadequacies, Hume is unable to make clear why, if we are confronted with what appears to be overwhelmingly strong evidence for some occurrence believed to be impossible, it must almost if not quite always be wrong to conclude that that event did after all occur and that we have been mistaken in believing it impossible. Hume does in fact concede that circumstances could arise in which we ought to admit the occurrence and therefore reject the proposition which previously we had believed to express a law of nature. But the rationale supplied is quite inadequate.

Suppose, Hume writes, that "all authors in all languages, agree that from the first of January 1600 there was a total darkness over the whole earth for eight days; suppose that the tradition of this extraordinary event is still strong and lively among the people; that all travelers who return from foreign countries bring us accounts of the same tradition without the least variation or contradiction—it is evident that our present philosophers, instead of doubting the fact, ought to receive it as certain and ought to search for the cause whence it might be derived."[37]

A more manageably plausible example can be produced by supposing that European astronomers, when word first reached them of the eclipse observations made centuries earlier in China, had been committed to a theory precluding the occurrence of any eclipses visible at any of the times or in any of the places listed in the Chinese records. Then, if there was no independent reason for suspecting the truth of those Chinese observations—no state ideology, for instance, to be supported by the occurrence of eclipses in those places and at those times—it would surely have been right for the European astronomers to have had very anxious second thoughts about the theory from which they had deduced that no eclipses could have been observed at the times and in the places recorded by their Chinese colleagues. They ought at the very least to have subjected that theory to every rigorous further test which they could think of. Yet, it would, surely, have been premature, instead of doubting the Chinese claims, to have received them as certain, and to have searched for the causes whence they might have been derived. The proper interim verdict on the historical problem would have been a baffled, and appropriately Scottish, "Not proven."

The crux here is again a matter of actual and possible evidence. The historical propositions, the propositions stating that an eclipse was visible in such and such a place at such and such a time, are all singular and in the past tense. It is always and necessarily too late now for any direct verification or falsification. If we are ever to discover what actually happened, then this can only be by finding something present which can be interpreted as evidence, and by assessing what and how much that available evidence shows.

It is altogether different with nomological propositions, propositions, that is, which state that causal connections or laws of nature obtain, and which necessarily imply something about practical necessity and practical impossibility. Nomological propositions are open and general. Also they can, at least in principle, be tested for truth or falsity at any time or in any place. Precisely that is why it is reasonable and right for the critical historian to employ all available confirmed nomologicals as canons of exclusion, ruling out many conceivable and even sometimes seemingly well-evidenced occurrences as practically impossible. Yet in doing this our historians should always be aware that steady advances in our knowledge of nomologicals, and occasional upsets revealing that what we have believed to constitute such knowledge was not, may demand historical reassessments—as in the cases of the supposed miracles of Vespasian and the alleged Phoenician circumnavigation of Africa.

As we have seen, Hume begins his discussion "Of Miracles" by expressing the confident hope that he is about to offer "an argument which . . . will . . . with the wise and learned be an everlasting check to all kinds of superstitious delusion." Certainly he would himself have rated the claims of parapsychology among those "impertinent solicitations" from which he was promising to free us. Equally certainly all the Founding

Fathers of what are now called parapsychological studies, and a great many of their successors, have been united in the hope of providing through such research "the preamble of all religions," and thus becoming able to proclaim, on empirical grounds, "that a spiritual world exists, a world of independent and abiding realities, not a mere 'epiphenomenon' or transitory effect of the material world."[38] Hume, therefore, would presumably have thought of parapsychology as—"like a considerable part of metaphysics"—no better than another robber lying "in wait to break in upon every unguarded avenue of the mind, and overwhelm it with religious fears and prejudices."[39]

The putative phenomena of parapsychology are best labelled, in a studiously theory-natural way, the psi-phenomena. This genus is then divided into two species: psi-gamma, and psi-kappa. The former includes all varieties of what used to be called Extrasensory Perception (ESP): telepathy, that is to say, and clairvoyance, whether retrocognitive, simultaneous, or precognitive. The latter is, in effect, a more noncommittal word for psychokinesis (etymologically, "movement by the mind").

It is usual to maintain that the phenomena, or the alleged phenomena, of parapsychology are, or would be, either nonphysical or even outright incompatible with physics. But what such psi-phenomena are or would be incompatible with is not, or not primarily, any particular named law of physics: Boyle's law, Gay Lussac's law, or what have you. Instead they do or would—as Hume liked to say—*violate* something far more universal and fundamental. What rules them out as impossible are some of what C. D. Broad identified as our "basic limiting principles," principles which together constitute a framework for all our everyday thinking about, and all our ordinary unphilosophical investigations of, human affairs, and principles which are continually being verified by our discoveries.

If, for instance, official secret information gets out from a government office, then the security people try to think of every possible channel of leakage; and what never appears on the check lists of such practical persons is psi-gamma. When similarly there has been an explosion in a power station or other industrial plant, then the investigators move in. At no stage will they entertain any suggestion that no one and nothing touched anything, that the explosion was triggered by some conscious or unconscious exercise of psi-kappa. Nor shall we expect them to turn up any reason for thinking that their, and our, framework assumptions were here mistaken.

It is, therefore, not surprising that skeptics have redeployed Hume's arguments as a challenge to the parapsychologists."[40] In 1955, for instance, *Science* published a paper by G. R. Price doing precisely that. This publication brought a strong response from Paul Meehl and Michael Scriven: "Price is in exactly the position of a man who might have insisted that Michelson and Morley were liars because the evidence for the physical theory of that time was stronger than that for the veracity of the experimenters."

It is most important to appreciate the reasons why this is not so. The first reason is that the Michelson–Morley experiment was *not* one member of a long series including many impressively disillusioning examples of fraud and self-deception. By contrast the history of parapsychology is full both of supposedly decisive demonstrations and of investigators of allegedly impeccable integrity which and who have later been exposed as fraudulent. Testimony in this area would appear to suffer all the corruptions believed by Hume to afflict the foundations of "systems of religion." For the issues are, in a more modern terminology, ideologically sensitive.

Second, there was in the Michelson–Morley case no reason at the time—nor has any such reason emerged since—to suspect that the experiment would not be repeatable, and repeated, as well as confirmed indirectly by other experiments similarly repeatable and repeated. But in parapsychology there are no regularly and reliably repeatable demonstrations. Indeed there is no regularly and reliably repeatable demonstration of the reality of any psi-phenomenon. (This is, incidentally, the reason—Pace Margaret Mead—why the Parapsychological Association ought never to have been permitted to affiliate to the American Association for the Advancement of Science, and should be expelled forthwith; unless, that is, affiliation is intended to be a tribute to scientific intentions rather than scientific achievement.)

Third, there is no even halfway plausible theory to account for the occurrence of psi-phenomena. This deficiency bears on the question of scientific status in two ways. For a theory which related the putative psi-phenomena to something else less contentious would tend both to probabilify their actual occurrence and to explain why they do thus indeed occur. Here we have the third reason why to refuse to accept the reality of such phenomena is not on all fours with dismissing the result of the Michelson-Morley experiment. For, even if no one then was ready immediately with an alternative theory, still in that case there was no good reason to fear that such a theory could not be produced. But in the case of parapsychology now, our investigators have had a hundred years for theoretical cogitation, from which labours they have as yet brought forth nothing even remotely persuasive.

These three objections reinforce one another. So, until and unless someone comes up with a reliably and regularly repeatable demonstration of some psi-phenomenon, we shall continue to have no sufficient reason to abandon any of those basic limiting principles which support the conclusion that all such phenomena are in fact impossible. All parapsychological reports will remain, and should continue to be treated as, miracle stories; just so many "accounts of miracles and prodigies" which, "as long as the world endures," will be "found in all history, sacred and profane." The most generous verdict upon any of this which can possibly be returned by a jury of wise men, who, as good Humeans, proportion their belief to the evidence—and would not even this verdict be too generous?—is that damping, and so appropriately Scottish, "Not proven!"

Notes

1. *Hume's Philosophy of Belief,* Antony Flew (London: Routledge and Kegan Paul, 1961).
2. *Enquiries concerning Human Understanding and concerning the Principles of Morals,* David Hume, ed. L. A. Selby-Bigge, 3d edition with text revised and noted by P. H. Nidditch (Oxford: Clarendon Press, 1975), p. v.
3. *Ibid.,* pp. xix and xviii.
4. *Ibid.,* pp. 12 and 11.
5. *English Thought in the Eighteenth Century,* Leslie Stephen, 3d edition (London: John Murray, 1902; reprint, New York: Peter Smith, 1949).
6. *Enchiridion Symbolorum,* H. Denzinger, 29th revised edition (Freiberg in Breisgau: Herder, 1953) sect. 1813.
7. *Philosophical Studies,* A. E. Taylor (London: Macmillan, 1934).
8. *Op. cit.,* p. 127
9. *Op. cit.,* p.179. F. H. Bradley. The first of these is reprinted in his *Collected Essays* (Oxford: Clarendon, 1935), Vol. I, pp. 1–70, while the second was first issued from the same press in 1946.
10. *An Introduction to the Philosophy of History,* W. H. Walsh (London: Hutchinson, 1951), pp. 106–7.
11. *Ibid.,* p. 88.
12. *Knowledge and Explanation in History,* R. F. Atkinson (London: Macmillan, 1978).
13. *Ibid.,* pp. 110–15.
14. *Ibid.,* p. 143.
15. *Ibid.,* p. 144.
16. This holds, of course, only of the causes of events which are not actions. Suppose that someone gives me good cause to celebrate, by reporting what is for me an excellent piece of news. They do not thereby ensure that I must make whoopee, willy-nilly. Causes, in this sense of "cause," incline but do not necessitate. Compare, for instance, particularly section 4 of "Hume and Historical Inevitability," chapter iii in my *A Rational Animal* (Oxford: Clarendon, 1978).

17. I have challenged Hume's account of the necessity of causes directly in "Another Idea of Necessary Connection" (*Philosophy,* 1982).
18. *Op. cit.* pp. 121-4.
19. *Ibid.,* pp. 124 and 344-6.
20. I *Corinthians* (xv) 14.
21. *Op. cit.,* pp. 128-9.
22. *Ibid.,* pp. 82 and 95
23. In "Inconsistency within a 'reconciling project'," published in *Hume Studies,* vol. iv (1978), I argue that Hume is here himself employing a notion of causal necessitation much stronger than anything for which he has made provision in his "so-called 'regularity' theory of causation."
24. *Op. cit.,* p. 114.
25. *Ibid.,* p. 114.
26. See, for instance, Max Black "Making Something Happen" in *Determinism and Freedom in the Age of Modern Science,* ed. S. Hook (New York: New York University Press, 1958); also reprinted in Black's *Models and Metaphors* (Ithaca, New York: Cornell University Press, 1962).
27. Compare, again, the article cited in note 17 above.
28. *Op. cit.,* p. 110.
29. 13 July, 1984. This letter was, by the way, a contribution to the controversy provoked by a newly appointed bishop of Durham. In the intervals between making a series of misinformed and egregiously uncharitable onslaughts upon the prime minister who had—presumably in a fit of absence of mind—recommended his appointment, this bishop was, it appears, expressing what were interpreted as his Christian unbeliefs: unbeliefs not only in the Virgin Birth, which is surely negotiable; but also in the Resurrection, which, for Pauline reasons, most categorically cannot be.
30. *Op. cit.,* p. 111; and compare section vi.
31. *Ibid.,* p. 110.
32. *Values in a Universe of Chance,* ed. P. P. Weiner (New York: Doubleday Anchor, 1985) pp. 292-3.
33. *Op. cit.,* book ii, part iii, sect. 1, pp. 404-5.
34. *Op. cit.,* p. 345.
35. For the relevant references compare *Hume's Philosophy of Belief,* pp. 183-4.
36. See book IV, chapter 42 of Herodotus's *History.*
37. *Op. cit.,* pp. 127-8.
38. These passages from the 1900 Presidential Address of the Society for Psychical Research (London) are, along with other similar

material, quoted in my "Parapsychology: Science or Pseudo-Science," first published both in the *Pacific Philosophical Quarterly,* vol. lxi (1980) and in M. P. Hanen, M. J. Osler and R. G. Weyant (Eds.) *Science, Pseudo-Science and Society* (Waterloo, Ontario: Wilfrid Laurier University Press, 1980); and also reprinted in P. Grim (Ed.) *The Occult, Science and Philosophy* (Albany, New York: SUNY Press, 1982).

39. *Op. cit.,* p. 11.
40. The references are given in the paper identified in note 38.

Donald Livingston

Hume's Conception

Of True Religion

Most discussions of Hume's philosophy of religion concentrate on the attack on religious beliefs and institutions that runs throughout Hume's philosophical and historical work. So strong is this focus that it has been easy to overlook the fact that Hume, himself, professed a religious outlook on the world which he variously describes as "philosophical theism," "true theism," and "true religion." These professions are usually played down as either ironic or, if genuine, as examples of Enlightenment deism, a view so devoid of religious significance as to be virtually identical with what today is known as atheism. Although some of Hume's religious affirmations are ironic, the "theistic" passages of *The Natural History of Religion,* the *Dialogues,* and other writings are genuine expressions of Hume's own sentiments.[1] Whether these have any religious significance is a deep question requiring a theory of what religion is and a frank recognition that our own religious con-victions or lack thereof will color any answer we may give. From the point of view of western theism, Hume's own theism does appear religiously empty, for he rejected the notion of a personal God who miraculously reveals himself in history. But then so does atheistic Buddhism, and it would seem extrava-gant to say that Buddhism is devoid of religious significance.

But before there can be any profitable discussion of the religious value of what Hume calls "true religion," we must have a clear picture of what he meant by it. This is not easy to arrive at because Hume does not discuss the notion of true religion in any depth in any one place. In what follows, I shall piece together Hume's scattered remarks on the subject. We shall find that "true religion," as Hume understands it, is not a pious gesture given to ingratiate himself to what was, in his own time, a largely religious audience but is an outlook central to his philosophical vision. Whether or not Hume's "true religion" has any religious value, it is, I shall argue, a notion crucial for understanding his philosophical achievement.

Hume taught in the first *Enquiry* that "religion . . . is nothing but a species of philosophy" (EU 146). So we cannot under-stand Hume's conception of religion without working through his conception of philosophy. Hume distinguishes between true and false philosophy, on the one hand, and true and false religion, on the other. As we shall see, true religion is a form of true philosophy; false religion is a form of false philosophy. In this section I discuss Hume's distinction between true and false philosophy, the parallel distinction for religion will be taken up in the remaining sections.

I have discussed elsewhere, at some length, Hume's reform in the traditional conception of philosophy.[2] Here I will only summarize the main features of Hume's reform. Philosophy, as traditionally conceived, is governed by two principles: the ultimacy principle and the autonomy principle. The ultimacy principle demands an understanding of the way things are in the light of the idea of ultimate reality. The autonomy principle requires that philosophy be a radically free and self-justifying inquiry. Anything less would reduce philosophy to the role of handmaiden of theology, politics, or some other prejudice. "Reason," Hume says "first appears in possession of the throne, prescribing laws, and imposing maxims, with an absolute sway and authority" (T 186). Hume accepted the ultimacy principle, but he deployed skeptical arguments to show that the autonomy principle, as traditionally conceived, is incoherent and, far from being a presupposition of philosophy, renders philosophy impossible.

The autonomy of philosophy (or of anything else for that matter) cannot be understood without understanding the heteronomous order relative to which it is supposed to be autonomous. In the case of philosophical inquiry this is common life, that *unreflectively* received order of habit, custom, prejudice, and tradition in which the philosopher originally lives and moves and has his being. The radical autonomy of philosophy requires that the philosopher deny original authority not simply to this or that prejudice of common life but to the whole order. The autonomous philosopher stands at an Archimedian point from which he may critically view the prejudices of common life as a whole. From this point of view, the whole unreflectively received order of common life is, as it were, presumed guilty until proven otherwise. The philosopher, as Hume has him say in the *Treatise,* cannot prevail with himself "to mix with such deformity" (T 264).

Hume argued that autonomous philosophy, if purged of the prejudices of common life, is not self-justifying, critical activity but, if consistently carried out, is self-destructive and ends in total skepticism. Philosophers, however, are seldom reduced to total doubt because they do not consistently adhere to the autonomy principle. Unknowingly, they smuggle in some favorite prejudice of common life which gives what is otherwise an entirely vacuous way of thinking authority and hides its fundamental emptiness.

If philosophical inquiry is to continue at all, it must reform itself by abandoning the autonomy principle in its pure form and by recognizing unreflective common life not as an object of critical reflection but as a category internal to its own critical activity. The true philosopher, then, is one who has seen through the emptiness of the autonomy principle and recognizes the independent authority of common life as a whole. But this does not mean that the true philosopher has abandoned critical reflection for philistinism. Having achieved critical reflection, he cannot go home again to a philosophically unreflective existence. Nor is common life an order of self-evident truths, as it was for commonsense philosophers such as Reid and G. E. Moore. Common life, for Hume, functions as a dialectical concept available only to philosophers who have painfully worked through to the vacuity of the autonomy principle and so are capable of seeing, for the first time, the independent authority that common life has for philosophical inquiry. In Hume's reform of philosophy, a revised version of the autonomy principle remains: philosophy may criticize any prejudice of common life by comparison with other prejudices of common life and in the light of abstract principles and ideals, but what it cannot do is achieve some Archimedian point from which to throw into question the order as a whole. The task of true philosophy, then, is to accept the prejudices of common life as one's own reality, to understand them, and to correct them: "philosophical decisions are nothing but the reflections of common life, methodized and corrected" (EU 162).

The true philosopher, then, has both an immanent and a transcendent existence relative to the world of common life. He exists within insofar as his thought presupposes the order. He exists without insofar as his thought is aimed at understanding ultimate reality. No prejudice of common life can fully satisfy the ultimacy principle, that is, the demand of thought to know the real. Yet it is only through these prejudices that we can think about the real. Skepticism, then, is not the enemy of true philosophy; rather it makes true philosophy possible: the true philosopher recognizes his cognitive alienation from ultimate reality but continues to inquire, though he has nothing but the "leaky weather-beaten vessel" of the prejudices of common life *through which* to think (T 263).

The false philosopher is not yet emancipated from the free play of the autonomy principle; he does not recognize the constitutive role that prejudice, custom, and tradition play in his own thought. Though necessarily a participant in common life, he is totally alienated from its authority by virtue of the autonomy principle. In its place he substitutes an alternative world which is pompously displayed as the work of autonomous reason but is, in fact, "the monstrous offspring" of reason and some favorite but unrecognized prejudice of common life. The false philosopher exists in a mode of false immanence and false transcendence. The alienated world of his own reason is alone considered real; yet the philosopher lives and moves and has his being in the order of common life which by the rationale of Descartes's evil demon hypothesis must, nevertheless, be viewed as a grand illusion. He exists within and without the world and can accept neither. Such a frame of mind can have no dwelling place in the world. From this tension arises the many forms of philosophic existence ranging from the extremes of a passive, bitter, and melancholy alienation from the world, as in the case of Diogenes, to implacably hostile and aggressive attempts to totally impose the alienated world of autonomous reason upon the world, as in the case of Marx. The false philosopher is either ridiculous or dangerous. From the perspective of Hume's "true philosophy," the figure of Diogenes must appear ridiculous as that of Marx must appear dangerous.

False philosophy is ridiculous and dangerous because it is

irrational. In conceptually eliminating the prejudices of common life, false philosophers can no longer make nonarbitrary distinctions of good and evil, true and false, *within* that order and so "no one can answer for what will please or displease them" (EM 343). Any criticism or acceptance of any part of common life will be arbitrary. Attempts at consistency must lead the false philosopher either to total asceticism or to total revolution. But neither action is coherent. The alienated ascetic philosopher can never free himself, psychologically or logically, from the prejudices of common life; he will forever, in Hume's expression, have "to mix with such deformity" (T 264). Nor is total revolution coherent, for, though the revolutionary may mutilate the world considerably, the alienated world that is to be imposed is empty, and without the prejudices of common life to give it content, no one can know whether it has been instantiated or not. But it is just these content-giving prejudices that were conceptually rejected in totality by false philosophy.

In the *Treatise* Hume remarks: "Generally speaking, the errors in religion are dangerous; those in philosophy only ridiculous" (T 272). This may suggest that religion is a threat to society, whereas philosophy is not. But this is not Hume's meaning, for he acknowledges, as the passage continues, that the errors of philosophy can be as dangerous as those of religion: "The Cynics are an extraordinary instance of philosophers, who from reasonings purely philosophical ran into as great extravagances of conduct as any *Monk* or *Dervise* that ever was in the world" (T 272). All the same, it is true that in the *Treatise* Hume tended to view the errors of philosophy as ridiculous affairs of the closet having little to do with the public world. His main concern is the theoretical one of marking the distinction between true and false philosophy, exposing the errors of the false and cultivating his own theory of human nature within the confines of the true. In two sections of the

Treatise, "Of the ancient philosophy" and "Of the modern philosophy," Hume views the western metaphysical tradition as dominated by the idea of substance which he pictures as an alienating form of false philosophy. Here Hume's conception of true philosophy is seen in the grand role of the self-critical culmination of the entire western philosophical tradition. The philosophers caught in the errors of this tradition are pictured not as a threat to society but as pathetic. They are, Hume says, in a "lamentable condition, and such as the poets have given us but a faint notion of in their descriptions of the punishment of *Sisyphus* and *Tantalus*" (T 223).

But in the first *Enquiry* and later works, he is eager to point out the threat that false philosophy poses to the peace of society. It is in the first *Enquiry* that Hume makes the claim that "religion . . . is nothing but a species of philosophy" (EU 146). The errors of religion are treated as philosophic errors. The Epicurean in the *Enquiry,* defending himself before the Athenians, and who may be taken to speak for Hume, attacks "the religious philosophers," not "the tradition of your forefathers and doctrine of your priests (in which I willingly acquiesce)" (EU 135). From the very first pages of the *Enquiry* on through to the famous book-burning passage at the end, Hume is militantly out to purge the alienating effects of false philosophy from the politics of common life. The "political interests of society," he says, have no "connexion with the philosophical disputes concerning metaphysics and religion" (EU 147). He insists on the "necessity of carrying on the war into the most secret recesses of the enemy" who "unable to defend themselves on fair ground, raise these intangling brambles to cover and protect their weakness. Chaced from the open country, these robbers fly into the forest, and lie in wait to break in upon every unguarded avenue of the mind" (EU 11-12).

Here the false philosopher, under the mantle of religion, is pictured as a highway robber threatening not the hearts of men but their *minds*. In the second *Enquiry*, Hume again uses the metaphor of the false philosopher as thief, but this time the philosopher is viewed as a purely secular theorist. Hume, accordingly, approves of the civil magistrate who places these "sublime theorists" who teach the equal distribution of property "on the same footing with common robbers" (EM 193). In the same work, Hume discusses Pascal as a modern, religious example and Diogenes as an ancient, secular example of how from purely philosophical arguments one can be led to an "artificial life" lived in total alienation from the common order. Hume presents such an existence as lived out not "in the air" of common life but "in a vacuum" and as the result of the illusions of "extravagant philosophy" and of "philosophical enthusiasm" (EM 341-43).

The "craft of popular superstition" was a common enemy for Hume and the Enlightenment generally. But Hume differed in thinking of religious superstition as continuous with philosophical thinking and as having the same rationale as the errors of ancient and modern metaphysics, none of which recognize the original authority of philosophically unreflective common life. Hume emerges, then, not as a child of the Enlightenment, but as its most searching adult critic. But a problem arises. If religion is but a species of philosophy, and its errors philosophic, what distinguishes religion from philosophy? And how can Hume say that religion and not philosophy is the primary threat to the peace of mind of the individual and society?

To answer these questions we must examine Hume's views on the historical origins of philosophy and religion. So far we have been talking about philosophy and religion as if they were timeless activities having certain conceptual relations—for instance, that religion is a species of philosophy. But the activities of philosophy and religion have developed over time and so their relations have not always been the same. Philosophy, for instance, developed historically out of religion and so has not always been a species of it. Hume's views on the origins of religious consciousness are presented in *The Natural History of Religion* and are well-known. I shall now briefly summarize them, weaving throughout the parallel natural history of philosophical consciousness which can be pieced together from Hume's remarks in *The Natural History of Religion* and other works.

Philosophy and religion have a common origin in the problem of causal understanding. Both are attempts to causally explain happenings in the world. Primitive man, confronted with the fearful chaos of life in which "life and death, health and sickness, plenty and want . . . are distributed amongst the human species by secret and unknown causes," attempts to form "ideas of those powers, on which we have so entire a dependence" (NHR 29). This search is governed by three original propensities of human nature. (1) The causes are arranged a priori into a *system*. Men would never have been led to continue the search for the causes of their destiny, especially after repeated failures, "were it not for a propensity in human nature, which leads into a system, that gives them some satisfaction" (NHR 29). (2) There is an original propensity to believe there is "invisible, intelligent power in nature" (NHR 38), and (3) a contrary propensity "equally strong to rest . . . attention on sensible, visible objects: and in order to reconcile these opposite inclinations, they are led to unite the invisible power with some visible object" (NHR 38). These propensities make possible not only primitive religion but also causal beliefs in metaphysics and modern science. Though original to human nature, they do not have the stability of such propensities as self-love, or affection between the sexes. Each of these is universal and has "always a precise determinate object, which it inflexibly pursues" (NHR 21). The three propensities which make religion, metaphysics, and theoretical science possible are "secondary." The objects and the strength of the propensities themselves are variable by critical reflection, and under certain extraordinary conditions can be altogether removed.

Polytheism was the first religion and the first system of causal explanation, the visible world being viewed as the effect of a system of warring and capricious deities. Popular theism arises out of polytheism not by recognizing the rational necessity of one supreme deity but out of the "adulation and fears of the most vulgar superstition." The polytheist worships his divinity out of fear, and in proportion as the fears become more urgent, new strains of adulation are invented until he arrives "at infinity itself, beyond which there is no farther progress" (NHR 43). And so out of fear and adulation, men stumble on to the idea of an all-perfect creator of the world, characterized by "unity and infinity, simplicity and spirituality" (NHR 47). But by virtue of the original propensity to invest intelligent causal power in visible objects, there is a permanent tendency in theism to collapse back into polytheism. The idea of an all-perfect spiritual being cannot be sustained without the notion of inferior mediators between man and the supreme deity. Partaking more of human nature, these middle beings gradually usurp the devotion due to the supreme being. There is, then, a dialectical tension in religion, what Hume calls a "flux and reflux," a tendency of polytheism to become theistic and a tendency of theism to collapse back into polytheism.

So far we have discussed the origin of popular theism. We have now to examine Hume's views on the nature of "philosophical theism," the form of theism that Hume himself accepts. In *The Natural History of Religion*, Hume says that "The whole frame of nature bespeaks an intelligent author; and no rational enquirer can, after serious reflection, suspend his belief a moment with regard to the primary principles of genuine Theism and Religion" (NHR 21). This basic belief that the universe is an intelligible system which expresses the mind of a single author is affirmed by Hume in many places.³ Philosophical theism has a different origin from that of popular theism and presupposes the prior cultivation of philosophical thinking. It is a belief that comes about only after men have acquired the settled tradition of making and correcting inductive inferences and of viewing nature in a lawlike way. When these historical conditions are satisfied, the three propensities mentioned earlier which gave rise to polytheism and vulgar theism are triggered and men acquire the belief in a single intelligent author of the universe.

Philosophical theism, though it has a natural origin (like polytheism and vulgar theism), is considered a rational belief of true philosophy. There is, however, a conceptual overlap between philosophical and vulgar theism. Traditional theists, says Hume, while "they confine themselves to the notion of a perfect being, the creator of the world, they concide, by chance, with the principles of reason and true philosophy; though they are guided to that notion, not by reason, of which they are in a great measure incapable, but by the adulation and fears of the most vulgar superstition" (NHR 43). The vulgar theist, like the first polytheists, is motivated to belief by fear. His is a miraculous and providential universe where God personally intervenes to accomplish his purposes. The philosophical theist is motivated to belief not by fear but by wonder and an appreciation of the lawlikeness of the universe. God, so conceived, is not a person who acts in history but is the "Sovereign mind or first principle of all things" who has "fixed general laws, by which nature is governed" (NHR 42, 75). It is the emancipation from fear and the emergence of a self-confident, contemplative, philosophic community that makes philosophical theism possible. But philosophical theism is also a belief constitutive of the community. Hume considered philosophical theism to be an absolute presupposition of the conceptual framework and methodology of scientific thought: "that nature does nothing in vain, is a maxim established in all the schools, merely from the contemplation of the works of nature, without any religious purpose" (D 214–15). That is, the belief is not the result of self-interested fear. Another theistic presupposition of science is to be found in "the Copernican system," the principle that "nature acts by the simplest methods, and chooses the most proper means to any end; and astronomers often, without thinking of it, lay this strong foundation of piety and religion. The same thing is observable in other parts of philosophy: And thus all the sciences almost lead us insensibly to acknowledge a first intelligent Author; and their authority is often so much the greater, as they do not directly profess that intention" (D 214–15).

Philosophy and religion, then, developed from the three original propensities which guide man's attempt to understand the world: the propensity to create a system of explanation, the propensity to project power or powers into the world, and the propensity to view the visible world symbolically as an expression of that power or powers. The difference is that the religious man is motivated by self-abnegating fear which is projected onto a fantasy world of voices whose commands he obeys. Philosophy emerges out of religion when men, somehow, gain confidence in their own judgments and become spectators of a world that is no longer infested with gods but is a world of wonder, beauty, and order to be grasped by the philosophic spectator's autonomous judgment. And it is this self-determining, autonomous judgment that philosopher's know as *reason*. The right order of the philosopher's soul is now seen as a symbol representing the right order of the cosmos, which is itself a representation of God's intelligence. The philosopher's existence, as philosophical theist, is characterized by Platonic, Aristotelian, and Augustinian *eros,* a longing desire for the wisdom possessed by God.

The emergence of reason is a liberating event in the history of mankind. The self-abnegation of polytheism and vulgar theism is transformed by the discovery of autonomous reason into the self-assertion of the philosophical theist. But not being properly understood, reason gives birth to a new form of enslavement: the autonomy principle of false philosophy. Autonomy and ultimacy properly belong to God's intelligence. But the claim of philosophy to autonomous reason meant that the philosopher's intelligence would be formally the same as God's. The dictates of the philosopher's own mind would result in an autonomous and ultimate world which, by virtue of the divinity of his own thought, must alone be considered real and which is contrary to the unreflectively received world of common life. Every object of experience and the whole of experience must appear double and contrary. The mark of reality must be given to the object of autonomous reason, but the contrary object of common life will claim its own reality which must be simultaneously satisfied and denied. The philosopher's mind is tortured by "two principles, which are contrary to each other, which are both at once embrac'd by the mind, and which are unable mutually to destroy each other" (T 215). Hume sees his own philosophy as accomplishing a further liberation for man by showing how the autonomy principle totally and absurdly alienates the philosopher from common life and by reforming the autonomy principle to include common life as a category of philosophical activity.

In *The Natural History of Religion,* Hume explored the curious beliefs and practices of popular religion and pictured them as "sick men's dreams" and "the playsome whimsies of monkies in human shape." Such passages have made Hume appear as the fire-eating child of the Enlightenment with a Manichean division of religion as darkness and philosophy as light. But we must remember that in the sections on ancient and modern philosophy in the *Treatise* (Book I, Part IV, Sections IV-V)

Hume pictures the entire tradition of western metaphysics as a bad dream brought on by the alienating effects of false philosophy. Metaphysical theories are pictured as responses to "spectres in the dark" and to "the punishment of Sisyphus and Tantalus" (T 223, 226). Superstition in false philosophy is different from superstition in religion, but it is superstition all the same.

When Hume says that religion is nothing but a species of philosophy, he is thinking of religion as a cognitive activity. Polytheism was the first consciously contrived cognitive system. Philosophical theism is the most developed cognitive system, functioning as the absolute conceptual framework within which modern science and true philosophy operate. But religion is more than a would-be cognitive activity. It has also functioned as a bond of social, moral, and political order. In *The Natural History of Religion,* Hume is concerned to expose the absurdity of religious practices and beliefs. But absurd religious practices may, nevertheless, have social utility, as Hume thinks many of them do. What Hume discovered, however, is that religious practices become more absurd and dangerous in proportion as they are captured by false *philosophical* thinking. And he observes that the more rational and philosophic a religion becomes, the more absurd are its practices: "all popular theology, especially the scholastic, has a kind of appetite for absurdity and contradiction" (NHR 54).

Hume held that popular theism is more rational than polytheism and naturally attracts a philosophical mind: "where theism forms the fundamental principle of any popular religion, that tenet is so conformable to sound reason, that philosophy is apt to incorporate itself with such a system of theology" (NHR 53). Polytheism is no longer philosophically appealing, so the most dangerous religion of all is a theistic religion embedded in a false philosophical system. The most developed form of this unholy alliance is the Christianity of modern Europe which, Hume thought, had been responsible for two centuries of political chaos and civil war. I turn now to an examination of how Hume conceives the history of this modern union of false philosophy and theism.

In barbarous times, before the appearance of philosophy, religious sects consisted of "traditional tales and fictions, which may be different in every sect, without being contrary to each other; and even when they are contrary, every one adhers to the tradition of his own sect, without much reasoning or disputation. But as philosophy was widely spread over the world at the time when Christianity arose, the teachers of the new sect were obliged to form a system of speculative opinions . . . and to explain, comment, confute, and defend, with all the subtlety of argument and science" (E 61). The union of philosophy and Christianity meant that Christianity would shatter into a hundred sects, just as philosophy had, and that these sects would stand in implacable opposition. The reason is that philosophy is governed by the principles of ultimacy and autonomy, and so the philosopher must view his own system as ultimate and the result of his own autonomous reason, which he cannot abandon without abandoning his self-integrity. Nor can he have patience with a contrary system which throws into question the worth of his very thought and existence.

Hume traces the hostility of philosophical opposition to an original propensity of the mind which is triggered whenever men reach the level of philosophical reflection on common life: "such is the nature of the human mind, that it always lays hold on every mind that approaches it; and as it is wonderfully fortified by an unanimity of sentiments, so it is shocked and disturbed by any contrariety. Hence the eagerness which most people discover in a dispute; and hence their impatience of opposition, even in the most speculative and indifferent opinions" (E 59). The philosophically reflective mind loves dominion. This is why *philosophical* sects were more fanatical in ancient times than religious sects. Hume observes: "Sects of philosophy in the ancient world, were more zealous than parties of religion; but, in modern times, parties of religion are more furious and enraged than the most cruel factions that ever arose from interest and ambition" (E 61). The reason for the transformation is that ancient pre-Christian religion had little or no philosophical content. Philosophical systems purport to provide an ultimate understanding of things. If taken seriously, total understanding leads to total control of every aspect of one's reality.

Hume explains this in the *Enquiry* on morals where he observes that in ancient times religion had "very little influence on common life" (EM 341). Men, having performed their duties in the temple, "the gods left the rest of their conduct to themselves, and were little pleased or offended with those virtues or vices, which only affected the peace and happiness of human society." It was, he continues, "the business of philosophy alone to regulate men's ordinary behaviour and deportment; and . . . this being the sole principle, by which a man could elevate himself above his fellows, it acquired a mighty ascendent over many, and produced great singularities of maxims and of conduct." In modern times, however, "philosophy has lost the allurement of novelty" and "has no such extensive influence; but seems to confine itself mostly to speculations in the closet; in the same manner, as the ancient religion was limited to sacrifices in the temple. Its place is now supplied by *the modern religion,* which inspects our whole conduct, and prescribes an universal rule to our actions, to our words, to our very thoughts and inclinations" (EM 341-43, emphasis added).

But we must keep in mind that the demand of modern religion for total dominion of body and soul, is due to the false philosophical thinking embedded in it. Ancient prephilosophic religion, in Hume's eyes, made no such demand. Hume discusses Diogenes as an ancient example and Pascal as a modern example of two thinkers in total alienation from common life. Both were caught in the grip of the illusions of false philosophy, what Hume calls "philosophical enthusiasm" and "extravagant philosophy," though the one expressed this in purely secular terms, the other in religious terms. What Hume said of the Stoics can be said of his view of modern Christianity, namely that it joins "a philosophical enthusiasm to a religious superstition" (NHR 63). The philosophical content of Christianity is especially strong in Protestantism which "being chiefly spiritual, resembles more a system of metaphysics" (H bk. IV: xxxviii, 12). But the theistic character of Christianity guarantees that all forms will be ordered, in some way, around a philosophical system and so will tend toward the domination of autonomous reason.

The philosophical impetus to dominion as expressed in modern religion extends beyond the body and soul of the individual to the social and political order as well. Because of this, Hume argues, a new sort of political party has emerged in modern times; namely, parties of metaphysical principle: "Parties from *principle,* especially abstract speculative principle, are known only to modern times, and are, perhaps, the most extraordinary and unaccountable *phenomenon* that has yet appeared in human affairs" (E 58). These are radically different from the traditional parties of interest and affection which are tied to visible goods of common life such as economic interest, ambition, and loyalty to persons and ruling households. Hume appears to have been the first to have recognized the modern phenomenon of metaphysical political parties. His deepest exploration of them is to be found in the volumes of *The History of England* dealing with the revolutionary events which occurred during the reign of the Stuarts.

Hume's treatment is prophetic. He viewed the English Civil War roughly in the way Burke viewed the French Revolution, not as a rebellion against oppression with which men of generous and liberal sentiments could sympathize, but as a war of metaphysical systems seeking instantiation. In Hume's hand the English Civil War becomes a case study of the nature and evil effects of false philosophy in politics. Hume is very clear that he considers the Puritan Revolution uniquely modern and an instructive lesson in philosophical error: "The gloomy enthusiasm which prevailed among the parliamentary party, is surely the most curious spectacle presented by any history; and the most instructive, as well as entertaining, to a philosophical mind" (H bk. V: lxii, 519). The entertainment and instruction Hume provides for the philosophical mind is to show that total alienation from common life and the demand of ultimacy and dominion that is the mark of false philosophy yields, in politics, total revolution and, finally, what we know today as totalitarian power.

The war, of course, was, in part, a religious one, but it was a war of "the modern religion" which has false philosophy built into it. And so there were not only conflicts over church doctrine and government but, most importantly, autonomous philosophical inquiries into the foundations of political authority. The "general humour of the time," Hume says, was "intent on plans of imaginary republics" (H bk. V: lix, 334). And again, "Every man had framed the model of a republic; and however new it was or fantastical, he was eager in recommending it to his fellow citizens, or even imposing it by force upon them" (H bk. V: lx, 386). In the first *Enquiry*, Hume had denied that "the political interests of society have any connexion with the philosophical disputes concerning metaphysics and religion" (EU 147). In the *History*, he shows that the political issues of common life were thrown into confusion by the antinomic reasoning of false philosophy: "The inquiries and debates concerning tonnage and poundage went hand in hand with these theological or metaphysical controversies (H bk. V: li, 58).

The conflict, as Hume conceived it, had nothing to do with this or that wrong that could be corrected by reform. The Puritan revolutionaries viewed the political order of common life not as the scene in which their own activities must operate but, in the manner of false philosophy, as an *object* of theoretical reflection: a complete system to be totally and all-pervasively replaced by an alternative system. The intention of the Commons, Hume writes, was "to subvert the whole system of the constitution" (H bk. V: lv, 196). Reform was out of the question. The Crown was helpless to placate "the endless demands of certain insatiable and turbulent spirits, whom nothing less will content than a total subversion of the ancient constitution" (H bk. V: liv, 163). Once men, through false philosophy, are conceptually emancipated from the existing social and political order, viewed now as a total system of prejudice, the usual judgments of right and wrong no longer apply. But the alternative world scheme, which is the work of autonomous reason, is empty; and without a guide from the prejudices of common life, anything may appear right or wrong, good or evil. The Puritans, Hume says, thought themselves "dispensed from all the ordinary rules of morality, by which inferior mortals must allow themselves to be governed." And again: the revolutionary principles were considered "superior to the *beggarly elements* of justice and humanity" (H bk. V: lx, 386). Hume sounds the theme, played out over and over with dreary repetition in the two centuries since, that total revolutions devour their children: "The sacred boundaries of the laws being once violated, nothing remained to confine the wild projects of zeal and ambition. And every successive revolution became a precedent for that which follow it" (H bk. V: lix, 330).

The revolution ended not in freedom from absolute government and an increase in liberty as the Puritans claimed but in an oppressive Puritan republic under the military dictatorship of Cromwell. "Never in this island was known a more severe and arbitrary government than was generally exercised by the patrons of liberty" (H bk. V: lix, 365). The Puritan regime sought to impose not only a different political constitution but a totally different social and moral order as well. Hume uses in the *History* the same image he had used in the *Treatise* and first *Enquiry* of the false philosopher as a robber of the things of common life. The Puritans were "sanctified robbers . . . who under pretence of superior illuminations, would soon extirpate, if possible, all private morality, as they had already done all public law and justice, from the British dominions" (H bk. V: lxii, 499). Common law was to be totally overthrown in favor of scriptural law to be interpreted by the elect. But some of the wilder factions thought that Christ had fully descended into the hearts of his saints and that the authority of all social institutions, including the Bible itself, were abolished (H bk. V: n. u, 554). Christians no longer were obliged to pay rent. A Quaker woman walks into Cromwell's presence naked because, among the elect, clothing must now appear as a mere prejudice.

When autonomous reason cuts itself loose from the prejudices of common life as a whole, we enter a hallucinatory, inverted world in which the reality of anything may be transformed into its opposite. Public nakedness is true modesty, property is theft, public law is illegality, and so on.

We are now in a position to interpret Hume's remark in the *Treatise* that the errors of religion tend to be dangerous, those of philosophy only ridiculous. He is not saying that philosophy is not dangerous. To the contrary, the religion that is dangerous is the institution of *modern religion* which has false philosophy built into it, and it is this false philosophical consciousness that twists religious tradition into grotesque and threatening shapes. False philosophy that has thrown off the mantle of religious tradition and appears in the public supported only by autonomous reason was, Hume thought, not sufficiently widespread to disrupt the politics of common life. For that to happen purely secular sects of false philosophy would have to become popular, and when he wrote the *Treatise,* Hume apparently thought that was as unlikely in the modern world as it was in the ancient.

In later works, however, as he examined more closely the nature of modern political parties, he came to see, with increasing alarm, that the distincitvely philosophical pattern of thought had indeed entered politics and on a popular level: "no party, in the present age, can well support itself without a philosophical or speculative system of principles annexed to its political or practical one" (E 452). Hume saw that those favorite eighteenth-century motives to political action—interest and ambition—had to be supplemented with a third: the desire for *philosophical* dominion. Hume first treated this intrusion of philosophical thinking into popular politics as amusing and harmless: "The people being commonly very rude builders, especially in this speculative way . . . their workmanship must be a little unshapely, and discover evident marks of that violence and hurry in which it was raised" (E 452). Hume even had hopes when he wrote the first *Enquiry* that the cultivation of philosophy could lead to wise political practice: "The stability of modern governments above the ancient, and the accuracy of modern philosophy, have improved, and probably will still improve, by similar gradations" (EU 10).

Hume remained in this state of guarded Enlightenment optimism about the relation of philosophy to politics until the British constitutional crisis that occurred in the last decade of his life. Hume saw the Wilkes and Liberty riots, the Bill of Rights movement, the general inchoate demand for democratic representation, and the demand of the radical Whigs that the monarchy be abolished in favor of a republic as threatening to throw the country into civil war. Nor were Hume's fears ungrounded. War had, indeed, broken out in the American colonies and had continued for over a year before Hume's death in August, 1776. Radical Whigs, who supported the Americans, viewed the conflict as a struggle for the British constitution on the fields of America. Hume saw no reason, therefore, to think that the civil war, already under way, could not erupt in Britain.

In rejecting a further extension of republican institutions in Britain, Hume was no reactionary. He supported total independence for the colonies as early as 1768 and always held to the republican ideal of government. But the ideal state is not necessarily the legitimate state, and Hume did not think historical conditions were right in Britain for abandoning constitutional monarchy. A pure republic, given British customs and traditions, would lead to anarchy and to the sort of oppressive republic imposed by Oliver Cromwell. "Such fools," he wrote his nephew in 1775, "are they, who perpetually cry Liberty: and think to augment it, by shaking off the Monarchy" (L bk. II: 306).

Hume interpreted the constitutional crisis of the last decade of his life as parallel to the crisis that led to the metaphysical struggle between Crown and Parliament which he had explored in the Stuart volumes. He interpreted both conflicts not as legitimate attempts at reform but as the hallucinatory result of false philosophy in politics. But whereas in the seventeenth century the demand for liberty was based on philosophical-religious theories, the demand in the late eighteenth century was based on philosophical-secular theories. If the crisis was ideological and evil, it was an evil due not to the clergy, that favorite enemy of the Enlightenment, but to philosophers who were now beginning to file out of Hume's closet for the public arena in great numbers.

Diderot wrote: "Let us hasten to make philosophy popular. If we want the philosophers to march on before, let us approach the people at the point where the philosophers are."[4] It never occurred to Diderot and to the *philosophes* generally (who were bemused by a Manichean-type division of religion as darkness and philosophy as light) that there might be a distinction between true and false philosophy and that an infusion of the latter into politics and on a popular level would be disastrous.

But near the end of his life, Hume began to see the threat that mass philosophical movements posed to politics, and this brought a chill to his relations with the French *philosophes,* whom he now began to see as dangerous. In a letter of 1769, he hoped that Abbe Morellet would deal adequately with the Physiocrats: "I hope that in your work you will thunder them, and pound them, and reduce them to dust and ashes!" And he wondered "what could engage our friend, M. Turgot, to herd among them" (L bk. II: 205). Hume found himself in disagreement with Turgot also over the value of Rousseau's writings which Hume considered to be "full of Extravagance and of Sophystry" and "whose general Tendency is surely to do hurt than Service to Mankind" (L bk. II: 91). Hume rejected Turgot's theory of "perpetual Progress towards Perfection" and the thesis "that the Encrease of Knowledge will still prove favourable to good Government" (L bk. II: 180), the very thesis he had tentatively put forth in the first *Enquiry* (EU 10). Hume presented, as a counterexample, the constitutional crisis in Britain symbolized by the Wilkes and Liberty riots. This crisis, Hume thought, was due entirely to the fanatical power of false philosophical consciousness, informed by that implacable triad of autonomy, ultimacy, and dominion. The crisis was not due to the superstition and ignorance of religion but to the Enlightenment itself. Hume makes this point clear in a letter to Hugh Blair. The Wilkes and Liberty affair, he says, "exceeds the Absurdity of Titus Oates and the popish Plot; and is so much more disgraceful to the Nation, as the former Folly, being derived from Religion, flow'd from a Source, which has, from uniform Prescription, acquir'd a Right to impose Nonsense on all Nations and all Ages" (L, II, 197). Philosophers in Hume's time were just beginning to claim that right. In our own time they would fully acquire it.

This is precisely the point made by Albert Camus in a famous passage of *The Rebel:* Distinguishing between "crimes of passion and crimes of logic," Camus writes:

> We are living in the era of . . . the perfect crime. Our criminals are no longer helpless children who could plead love as their excuse [Hume's parties of interest and affection]. On the contrary, they are adults, and they have a perfect alibi: philosophy, which can be used for any purpose—even transforming murderers into judges. . . . In more ingenuous times, when the tyrant razed cities for his own greater glory . . . the mind did not reel before such unabashed crimes, and judgment remained unclouded. But slave camps under the flag of freedom, massacres justified by philanthropy . . . in one sense cripple judgment. On the day when crime dons the apparel of innocence through a curious transposition peculiar to our times—it is innocence that is called upon to justify itself.

Hume appears to have been the first modern philosopher to understand this "curious transposition" of concepts to which Camus refers and to demand what seemed unthinkable, namely, that philosophy, *as such,* should explain and justify herself before the tribunal of common life. Philosophical consciousness supposes that all concepts constructed by autonomous reason are ultimate and worthy of dominion. The Humean inquisition in politics proceeds by the rule that political concepts constructed by the philosophical imagination such as liberty, equality, human rights, the class struggle, social justice are guilty until proven innocent.

The self-conscious political world in which we live is very much a world of contrary *philosophical* systems seeking instantiation in the world: liberalism, conservatism, fascism, socialism, Marxism, communism, feminism, and on and on. Of all these, the Humean question must be asked of whether the philosophy that informs them is the true or the false. False philosophy is, of course, the more compelling and is so firmly entrenched in popular political-philosophical consciousness that it is easy to overlook the insight Hume won into the nature of its error. It may therefore help to examine a few examples of the error in its starkest form.

The most rigorous form of the autonomy principle is to be found in Descartes who proposed, as a matter of method, the conceptual elimination of the prejudices of common life in favor of an alternative order conforming to the self-imposed dictates of autonomous reason. Comparing the prejudices of common life to an old house, Descartes has Eudoxus say in *The Search After Truth:* "I know no better remedy than absolutely to rase it to the ground, in order to raise a new one in its stead. For I do not wish to be placed amongst the number of these insignificant artisans, who apply themselves only to the restoration of old works, because they feel themselves incapable of achieving new."[5] The Cartesian conception of reason lingers on in the popular and supposedly self-evident maxim that just because something is a custom or tradition is no reason to continue it. That is, custom or tradition, as such, can never be a reason for doing anything. Descartes realized that this conception of reason required total revolution and ruled out reform, and, being conservative politically, he was anxious to insist that it applied only to natural science, mathematics, and metaphysics and should be quarantined from politics and morals.[6] But this was clearly an arbitrary move. Besides, Descartes was only making explicit the radical autonomy implicit in philosophy from its inception and which Hume set out to reform.

It should not be surprising, then, that a century and a half after Descartes's death, when philosophical consciousness had spread to the middle classes, that a member of the National Assembly, during the French Revolution, could address his colleagues not with the language of reform but with the Cartesian language of total criticism: "All the establishments in France crown the unhappiness of the people: to make them happy they must be renewed, their ideas, their laws, their customs must be changed . . . men changed, things changed, words changed . . . destroy everything; yes, destroy everything; then everything is to be renewed."[7] We have here something very like the inverted world of the Puritan revolutionaries. The same inversion is to be found in Rousseau's famous remark that "man is born free but everywhere he is in chains" and that man must be "forced to be free." It is to be found in Proudhon's thesis that "property is theft," and in Charles Fourier's demand for total revolution: "the vice of our so-called reformers is to indict this or that defect, instead of indicting civilization as a whole, inasmuch as it is nothing but a vicious circle of evil in all its parts; one must get out of this hell."[8] The early Marx wrote that his criticism of society was not against "wrong in particular" but against "wrong in general." The task was not to reform society but to totally change it. Marx makes this clear in his address of 1850 to the Communist Party on tactics: "We are not interested in a change in private property but only in its annihilation, not in conciliation of class antagonisms but in the abolition of classes, not in reforms of present society but in the foundation of a new one."[9] To these examples we may add the various contract theories of government proposed by Hobbes, Locke, Rousseau, Kant, and Rawls. These seek to determine what our political rights and duties are not by embracing, living through, and correcting the prejudices of common life from within, but by reference to standards we would have chosen in an Archimedean position of equality outside of common life. Contract theorists typically do not call for total revolution, but they follow Descartes' method in *conceptually* destroying the prejudices of common life as a whole. But with these methodologically eliminated, there is no nonarbitrary way to give content to the abstract and empty contract principles and so anything may appear to sat-isfy or violate them. Total revolution is logically as acceptable as total acceptance of the status quo. What keeps the contract theorist from either extreme is the presence of unrecognized prejudices of common life in his own soul.

One may at this point raise an objection. Surely, one might say, there is some truth in the examples of false philosophy in politics mentioned above. Is there not some truth in the French Revolution, the criticism of Rousseau, the contract theory, Marx? The Humean reply to this would be that there is no truth at all in the inverted-world-type thinking of false philoso-phy. Whatever truth there is to these theories when applied to the world is due to unrecognized prejudices of common life which secretly enter to guide and give the theories whatever content they contain or to pragmatic compromises with the prejudices of common life.

Less than a century after Hume first observed that "no party, in the present age, can well support itself without a philosophi-cal or speculative system of principles annexed to its political or practical one" (E 452), Marx wrote that "the philosophical consciousness itself has been pulled into the torment of strug-gle" and that what must be accomplished is "the *ruthless criticism of all that exists,* ruthless also in the sense that criticism does not fear its results and even less so a struggle with the existing powers."[10] The alienated demand of false philosophy for auton-omy, ultimacy, and dominion is here fully manifest. Michael Oakeshott once observed that everything Marx touched turned to superstition.[11] We are now in a position to give a Humean interpretation of Oakeshott's observation. For Hume, supersti-tion in modern religion is due to the alienating effects of false philosophy. The superstitious man and the false philosopher alike bracket out the prejudices of common life as a whole in favor of an alternative world, what Hume calls "a world of its own," presenting "us with scenes, and beings, and objects, which are altogether new" (T 271). This dream world, alone, has the title of reality, and the world of common life is seen as an illusion. The superstitious man and the false philosopher exist in both worlds but can accept neither. The essence of superstition, then, is the transformation of common life or a significant part of it into the category of illusion. Thus Proudhon's statement that "property is theft" is a case of superstition because it transforms the entire order of property relations into an illusion. Likewise the contract theory from Hobbes to Rawls is superstitious because it methodologically requires that we bracket out the entire traditional political order as having no authority at all to determine political principles. The superstition in Marx that Oakeshott has put his finger on is not a quirk of Marx's thinking but is due entirely to the pattern of false philosophy which has plagued modern political thought from its inception. We have seen Hume use the image of the false philosopher as a man with bad dreams and as a thief. He also uses the image of a worker in black magic. In the second *Enquiry,* for instance, the false philosopher is presented as an alchemist who through "Philosophical chemistry" transforms parts of common life into illusions (EM 297). And in the essay "The Sceptic," Hume clears the air of false philosophy with this rhetorical question: "Do you come to a philosopher as to a *cunning man,* to learn something by magic or witchcraft, beyond what can be known by common prudence and discretion?" (E 163).

Hume held that the antidote to false religion and to false philosophy is true philosophy (EU 12). But we must now see how true religion, for Hume, is built into the nature of true philosophy, and how the true philosopher and the true religious man are the same. A glimpse of this is already available in Hume's doctrine of philosophical theism which unites true philosophy and religion on the question of causal understanding.

Philosophical theism is the most developed form of causal reasoning, and the belief that the universe is a system which is the result of purposive intelligence is a belief constitutive of the scientific community. It is because of his own adherence to philosophical theism that Hume could scandalize the polite atheists at Holbach's dinner party by insisting that he had never met a true atheist.[12]

But religion, whether polytheistic or theistic, is more than an attempt at causal understanding. It has also functioned as a bond of social and political order, and so the question of its social utility arises. Philosophically unreflective common life is an order of customs, prejudices, and traditions. One task of religion has been to hold this order together, not by causal understanding but by praising its *sacred* character. The religious man, then, views himself as part of a sacred ordering of things which he is able to affirm and celebrate to the extent that he possesses the virtue of *piety*. Hume praised the prephilosophic polytheistic religions of the ancient world for their social utility. Philosophy, however, as traditionally conceived (that is, on Hume's view, false philosophy), is a threat to any social order, because, as we have seen, false philosophy always has the effect of transforming the whole or a significant part of common life into illusion. The true philosopher, however, recognizes the prejudices and traditions of common life as having original authority and as a limit within which reason must operate on pain of its own self-destruction. If we may think of the sacred as, at the very least, that over which autonomous reason has no authority, then common life is, for Hume, a sacred order. Common life is a mysterious, awesome, and radiant world which false philosophy with its alienating demand of autonomy, ultimacy, and dominion cannot penetrate. The true philosopher, then conceives of himself as part of a sacred ordering of things (common life as a whole), which is, at the same time, a condition without which genuine philosophical reflection is impossible; and this means that the true philosopher, as such, must have the virtue of piety. Reverence for the sacredness of our common order is essential to Hume's reformation of philosophy.

Hume explains the task of true religion this way: "The proper office of religion is to regulate the heart of men, humanize their conduct, infuse the spirit of temperance, order, and obedience; and as its operation is silent, and only enforces the motives of morality and justice, it is in danger of being overlooked. . . . When it distinguishes itself, and acts as a separate principle over men, it has departed from its proper sphere, and has become only a cover to faction and ambition" (D 220). Religion becomes false for the same reason that philosophy does, namely when the object of its thought is alienated from common life and becomes "a separate principle over men." True religion, as a passion of piety immanent in common life, provides a motive for keeping philosophy within its proper bounds. The impiety which had always plagued philosophy and Christianity, too, was becoming worse in what Hume disdainfully called "this philosophic age." And so Hume had occasion to observe a new order of men rendered impious not by Christian false philosophy but by secular philosophy: "There is a new set of men lately sprung up amongst us, who endeavour to distinguish themselves by ridiculing every thing, that has hitherto appeared sacred and venerable in the eyes of mankind. Reason, sobriety, honour, friendship, marriage, are the perpetual subjects of their insipid raillery; and even public spirit, and a regard to our country, are treated as chimerical and romantic" (E 573). Hume describes this new set of men as "anti-reformers." They are the false philosophers we have already examined for whom reform is out of the question and who, by the unrestrained use of the autonomy principle, twist ordinary beliefs and practices of common life into their opposites: benevolence is really self-love, property is really theft, civility is true barbarity, and so on.

In the *Treatise*, Hume shows how the entire world of human culture may be viewed as a religious ritual. Hume discovered the performative use of language which J. L. Austin was later to exploit so brilliantly. Language not only describes the world it also *constitutes* the specifically human world. When used in ritual acts language actually creates a nonnatural world of objects and relations such as marriage, property, law, government, manners, and the entire hierachy of status, rank, and authority among men. The world-making power of ritualistic language is, Hume says, "one of the most mysterious and incomprehensible operations that can possibly be imagin'd, and may even be compar'd to *transubstantiation,* and *holy orders,* where a certain form of words, along with a certain intention, changes entirely the nature of an external object" (T 524). Hume gives an example: "Had I worn this apparel an hour ago, I had merited the severest punishment; but a man, by pronouncing a few magical syllables, has now rendered it fit for my use and service" (EM 199).

The common life of man, then, is a fragile structure of nonnatural relations held together by the symbolic and ritualistic use of language. Man without ritual is impossible. But Hume makes a distinction between true and false ritual: "'tho these mysteries [justice and superstition] be so far alike, 'tis remarkable, that they differ widely in other particulars" (T 524). True rituals serve the interests of common life; whereas false rituals serve the interests of the alien reason of false philosophy. False rituals, whether in modern religion or modern politics, constitute an alien world that is both parasitic upon and exists at the expense of common life. False rituals have two ill effects. First, the power of the ritual to transform a natural object into a moral object is mistaken for a *causal power* to transform a natural object into a supernatural object. Second, true ritual serves the interests of common life which are historical, fluid, and changing; it, therefore, is "warp'd into as many different forms as that interest requires, and even runs into direct contradictions, rather than lose sight of its object" (T 524). False ritual serves the interests not of common life but of "a separate principle over men" and so tends to be systematic, consistent, inflexible, and oppressive. The true religious man can have no special system of rituals to which reverence is due, because the whole of common life is the set of rituals to which reverence is due.

We must now see how common life, as an order of sacred ritual, is connected to philosophical theism. Common life is seen as a gift, the result of a mysterious providence. The "profound adoration" which Philo has for the "divine Being" issues in an affirmation and love of the order of common life as it is. This Humean affirmation of the world (by contrast with the world-changing thought of false philosophy such as Marxism) is not to be confused with a smug acceptance of the status quo. We have seen, repeatedly, that Hume's conception of true philosophy has the necessity of reform built into it. The providential affirmation of common life serves merely the purpose of keeping philosophy within its proper bounds. But a problem arises, for Hume rejects the traditional notion of providence, where God is viewed as a person who reveals his particular purposes in nature and in history. What content, then, can the idea of providence have for Hume?

The answer must be that Hume allows very little content to the idea, but it is not entirely empty. In the *Dialogues,* Hume argues that no inductive argument for God's existence can be conclusive. Philosophical theism, however, is a natural belief and not the result of inductive reasoning. In this respect, it is like belief in external objects and causal connections which are also on Hume's view, incapable of inductive support. But though philosophical theism is not the result of inductive reasoning, its content must be specified by analogy with human experience. And Hume finds the resemblance between human and Divine nature so weak as to render any understanding of God's nature limited in the extreme. The result is the idea of

God as purposive intelligence, what Philo calls "MIND OR THOUGHT" (D 217). But God's purposes are mysterious and cannot be rationally discerned in either history or nature. Hume treats all attempts of religious philosophers to penetrate this providence as impiety (D 281). But such attempts also lead. to superstition. False philosophy, with its implacable demand for autonomy, ultimacy, and dominion, must, impiously, transform God into an object of its own appropriation. And when this happens, the idea of the creator, himself, will be used to transform the whole or a significant part of common life into illusion. Hume's efforts to expose the absurdity of all attempts by philosophers to know the particular workings of providence, either through revelation or natural theology, is not designed to destroy the theistic conception of the universe but, rather, to determine what the philosopher's relation to the divinity is.

The philosopher's mind is not cognate with the divine mind. Consequently, the radical demands of autonomy, ultimacy, and dominion are not properly features of the philosopher's mind but belong to the divinity. And this is just another way of stating Hume's reform in philosophy: that the philosopher's thought is not autonomous, that it has no claim to be ultimately true, and that power must be shared.

Ernest Campbell Mossner has suggested that the religion Hume embraces is "the religion of man."[13] "Humanism" has many meanings, many of which are compatible with theism of various forms. But if we mean by "humanism" the transubstantiation of divinity into man whose perfectibility is the highest value, then Hume is no humanist; for that would mean reading the logic of the idea of divinity into man. Marx is such a humanist. In his doctoral dissertation of 1840–41, he writes: "Philosophy does not make a secret of it. The confession of Prometheus: 'In one word, I hate all the gods,' is its very own confession, its own sentence against all heavenly and earthly gods who refuse to recognize human self-consciousness as the supreme divinity—by the side of which none other shall be held."[14] The philosophical transformation of human self-consciousness into divinity, as seen in the work of such post-Enlightenment thinkers as Hegel, Comte, and Marx, would surely be viewed by Hume as cases of what he called "philosophical enthusiasm" and would be splendid specimens for an expanded and up-to-date version of *The Natural History of Religion.* Hume's vision of the universe and of philosophy is still firmly rooted in the theistic tradition.

But, as we have seen, Hume's theism is a belief internal to the philosophical community and quarantined as far as possible from the popular theistic tradition. There is a question, however, which arises within Hume's theory of natural belief which the advocate of popular theism will surely pose. If Hume is prepared to accept philosophical theism as a historically determined natural belief, it is hard to see why he can find no truth in the writings and rituals which constitute the theistic tradition. And it will not do to say that these writings violate a priori and inductive canons of thought because Humean natural beliefs in physical objects, causal connections, and personal identity are also incoherent by these standards. One of Hume's great achievements was to have shown how "fictions" of the imagination (fictions, that is, relative to a priori and inductive canons) can be bearers of truth about reality. In the Introduction to the *Treatise,* Hume says that "we can give no reason for our most general and most refined principles, beside our experience of their reality" (T xxii). We just find ourselves with experiences of external objects, causal connections, the personal identity of ourselves and others, and the universe as the result of purposive activity—though we cannot render these experiences coherent by a priori or inductive reason. What we can do is frankly recognize this fact, give a historical account of the origins of the experiences and critically examine the beliefs embedded in them for their cognitive content.

It is remarkable that, of the four major experiences (mentioned above) that constitute the outline of our world, most of Hume's effort is directed to distilling the truth from man's theistic experiences. Hume devoted two books to this analysis. *The Natural History of Religion* and *The Dialogues Concerning Natural Religion* jointly constitute a history of the origins of theistic experience in human nature and a critical analysis of the cognitive content of that experience. No comparable effort was extended to an analysis of the other founding experiences. In particular, no such effort was directed to an analysis of our causal experience. There Hume was content to show that our causal experience of the world is rooted in human nature, not reflection, and that it is mediated by fictions of the imagination that we share with animals. Having secured inductive practice in human nature, the rationale of Hume's insight demanded that he go on to an examination of the history of the higher inductive practices and order-making fictions of the imagination in the theoretical science of his time just as, in *The Natural History of Religion,* he had shown how primitive polytheistic experience developed into vulgar theism and, through the mediation of philosophical experience, into philosophical theism. In short, the rationale of Hume's conception of causal experience demands a *Natural History of Scientific Judgment* roughly on the order of *The Natural History of Religion.* Thomas Kuhn's *The Structure of Scientific Revolutions* would be a good example of the sort of book demanded by a fully developed Humean conception of causal experience.

But if the fictions of the imagination are bearers of truth about external objects, causal connections, personal identity, and if the inductive habits of the scientific community are bearers of truth about philosophical theism, then one might wonder why the traditions of popular theism may not be bearers of truth about the God of philosophical theism. In this way, the thinly populated idea of philosophical theism could perhaps be given a richer content. Philo raises just this possibility in his confession of belief in philosophical theism at the end of the *Dialogues*. He laments the fact that the philosophical understanding of God is through imperfect analogy and "can be carried no farther than to the human intelligence; and cannot be transferred, with any appearance of probability, to the other qualities of the mind" (D 227). And then he adds: "Some astonishment indeed will naturally arise from the greatness of the object: Some melancholy from its obscurity: Some contempt of human reason, that it can give no solution more satisfactory with regard to so extraordinary and magnificent a question. But . . . the most natural sentiment, which a well-disposed mind will feel on this occasion, is a longing desire and expectation, that Heaven would be pleased to dissipate, at least alleviate, this profound ignorance, by affording some more particular revelation to mankind. . . . A person, seasoned with a just sense of the imperfections of natural reason, will fly to revealed truth with the gratest avidity" (D 227).

Hume is not a fideist, and he saw no truth in revealed religion, but the above passage well expresses the logic of his position. Philosophical theism, as a natural belief, *is* accompanied with a feeling of longing and emptiness. The content of philosophical theism is austere, and the vulgar are incapable of "so pure a religion as represents the Deity to be pleased with nothing but virtue in human behavior" (D 221). Philosophical theism must lie under the "inconvenience, of being always confined to very few persons" (D 223). And even philosophers cannot long be content with an abstract conception of God anymore than they can be content with an abstract conception of external objects, causal connections, and personal identity. The mind will infuse these notions with some imaginary content. In the above passage about the necessity of revealed religion, Philo is registering this fact of human nature, as does Hume in "The Sceptic": *Philosophical devotion . . .* like the enthusiasm of a poet, is the transitory effect of high spirits, great leisure, a fine genius, and a habit of study and contempla-

tion" (E 170). But the abstract objects of philosophical reflection cannot long actuate the mind. "To render the passion of
continuance, we must find some method of affecting the senses
and imagination, and must embrace some *historical* as well as
philosophical account of the Divinity. Popular superstitions and
observances are even found to be of use in this particular" (E
170).

Hume treats the imaginary content of the other founding
experiences as bearers of truth not barriers to it. But he does
not extend this reading to the rituals and practices of the theistic
tradition. Nowhere does Hume treat the Bible as a product of
the imagination which can be interpreted as revealing truth
about man and God. Any truth in the Bible is better expressed
in the pagan philosophers and moralists.

But the popular theist may claim that Hume has arbitrarily
selected a narrow range of human experiences to investigate.
Hume's own understanding of theism was restricted to the
experience of the scientific community and to the morality of
civil society. A broader range of experiences, including biblical
experiences, might have yielded a richer form of theism. There
is something to this criticism. Hume's historical provinciality,
like that of many Enlightenment thinkers, is, at times, appall-
ing. Not only are the biblical and medieval traditions her-
meneutically opaque, the experiences of barbarous people
generally are cast into outer darkness. Hume for instance,
begins the *History of England* not with the barbarous Britons but
with the appearance of the civilized Romans on the grounds
that "the adventures of barbarous nations, even if they were
recorded, could afford little or no entertainment to men born in
a more cultivated age . . . and it is rather fortunate for letters
that they are buried in silence and oblivion" (H bk. I: 1). Hume
lacked a hermeneutical principle for interpreting mythic writings, and so the biblical literature of popular theism remained
unintelligible. Nevertheless, Hume's doctrine that the fictions
of the imagination have cognitive significance (a doctrine

which he exploited in his analysis of scientific experience and the experience of civil society) opens the way to a theory of how mythical consciousness can have cognitive significance. But Hume, himself, never entered it.

Hume's failure to penetrate the biblical literature and rituals of popular theism and to ask whether, if purged of false philosophy, they could be bearers of truth, should not detract from his great achievement, which was to have discovered the illusion-making activity of false philosophy and to have exposed the evil it had wrought in Christianity. We may observe that Christianity today has largely shed the implacable demands of false philosophy for autonomy, ultimacy, and dominion and has incorporated itself peaceably into civil society. Relations between Christian sects more closely resemble the pluralism of those polytheistic, prephilosophic religions of antiquity which Hume praised than the implacable opposition of the *philosophical* sects of antiquity which he condemned. This change in the Christian tradition appears to be due to its experience of the Enlightenment and to the sort of criticism Hume launched. But, as Hume taught, Christianity is a modern religion with philosophy built into it, and so there is a permanent tendency in Christianity to slip back into the errors and impiety of false philosophy.

The same tendency, however, exists for true philosophy and true religion. The tendency of philosophical reflection to alienation from common life is overwhelming. The perspective of true philosophy and the passion of true religion attendant upon it are rare and fragile achievements in any case but especially under modern conditions where philosophy has become popular. Under such conditions, the tendency of philosophy to become false, to construct an alternative world, and to constitute it with rituals of its own making is irresistible. Hume seems to teach what might be called the principle of the conservation of superstition, that the quantity of philosophic and religious superstition is constant and merely changes forms from time to time. Hume points out, pessimistically, that even if true religion were to become established so that there should be a popular institution that preached only morality and reason, "so inveterate are the people's prejudices, that, for want of some other superstition, they would make the very attendance on these sermons the essentials of religion, rather than place them in virtue and good morals" (NHR, 70-71). So strong is the drive of philosophical consciousness to substitute a fantasy world, structured by rituals of its own making, for the world of common life! Modern liberal and socialist political ideologies which have dominated the twentieth century may be viewed as cases of just such a religion. Their content is, officially, purely moral and rational. But whatever truth these ideologies may contain (and being connected to common life, they must contain some truth), the ritualistic behavior of their false philosophical content has generated as much suffering in the world as the most grotesque religious superstition. Humean true philosophy brings to light the original authority of unreflective common life and, in the light of it, places a constraint on all philosophical theorizing. Humean true religion teaches love of this unreflective order and prohibits all attempts at *salvation* from it, whether philosophical or religious.

Notes

Abbreviations of Hume's works cited in the text are as follows.

T: *A Treatise of Human Nature,* ed. L. A. Selby-Bigge, 2nd edition with text revised and variant readings by P. H. Nidditch (Oxford: Clarendon Press, 1978)

EU: *Enquiries Concerning Human Understanding and*

EM: *Concerning the Principles of Morals,* ed. L. A. Selby-Bigge, 3d edition revised by P. H. Nidditch (Oxford: Clarendon Press, 1975)

E: *Essays, Moral, Political, and Literary* (Oxford: Clarendon Press, 1966)
   NHR: *The Natural History of Religion*, ed. H. E. Root (London: Adam and Charles Black, 1956)
D: *Dialogues Concerning Natural Religion*, ed. Norman Kemp Smith (Indianapolis: Bobb Merrill, 1947)
H: *The History of England, From the Invasion of Julius Caesar to the Abdication of James the Second*, 1688, with the author's last corrections and improvements. 6 vols. (Boston: Phillips Sampson, 1854)
L: *The Letters of David Hume*, ed. J. Y. T. Grieg, 2 vols. (Oxford: Clarendon Press, 1969)

1. *Dialogues*, p. 214; *The Natural History of Religion*, p. 21; *Treatise*, p. 633n; and Hume's *A Letter from a Gentleman to His Friend* in Edinburgh, ed. Ernest Campbell Mossner and John V. Price (Edinburgh: University of Edinburgh Press, 1967), pp. 24-26.

2. See chapters one and two of my *Hume's Philosophy of Common Life* (Chicago: University of Chicago Press, 1984).

3. *Dialogues*, p. 214; *The Natural History of Religion*, p. 21; *Treatise*, p. 633. For further support for the thesis that Hume accepted some form of theism, see George J. Nathan, "The Existence and Nature of God in Hume's Theism," in *Hume: A Re-Evaluation*, ed. Donald Livingston and James King (New York: Fordham University Press, 1976), pp. 126-49, and Keith E. Yandell, "Hume on Religious Belief" in *Hume A Re-Evaluation*, pp. 109-25.

4. Quoted in Ernst Cassier, *The Philosophy of the Enlightenment*, trans. Fritz C. A. Koelln and James P. Pettegrove (Boston: Beacon Press, 1955), pp. 268-69.

5. Rene Descartes, *The Philosophical Works of Descartes*, trans. Elizabeth S. Haldane and G. R. T. Ross (Cambridge: Cambridge University Press, 1969), Vol. I, p. 313.

6. Descartes, I, p. 90.

7. Quoted in Edmund Burke, *Reflections on the Revolution in France*, ed. Thomas Mahoney (Indianapolis: Bobbs Merrill, 1982), p. 196.

8. Charles Fourier, *Oeuvres completes*, 6 vols. (Paris, 1846-48), 6:xv.

9. Quoted in Eric Voeglin, "The Formation of the Marxian Revolutionary Idea," *The Review of Politics*, XII, p. 301.

10. *Karl Marx on Revolution*, 13 vols., ed. and trans. Saul K. Padover (New York: McGraw-Hill, 1971), I, p. 516.

11. Michael Oakeshott, *On Human Conduct* (Oxford: Clarendon Press, 1975), p. 309.

12. The affair is discussed in Ernest Campbell Mossner, *The Life of David Hume* (Oxford: Clarendon Press, 1980), p. 483.

13. Ernest Campbell Mossner, "The Religion of David Hume," *The Journal of the History of Ideas,* 39, pp. 653-63.
14. Quoted in Eric Voeglin, "The Formation of the Marxian Revolutionary Idea."

George I. Mavrodes

Revelation

And the Grounding of Faith

Many theologians and philosophers of religion have made a distinction between *natural religion* and *revealed religion*. Maybe this distinction is useful for some purpose. In any case, Christianity makes such heavy use of the concept of *revelation*, and of related notions, such as those of *God's speaking to the prophets, God's coming into the world in the incarnation*, and so on, that it would seem to be a prime example of a revealed religion. Or if we wish to serve notice that we are not yet ready to accept Christianity's claim that it has a genuine revelation, we could at least say that Christianity seems to understand itself as a revealed religion. That seems to be the way in which Christians characteristically understand the basis of their own faith. And it would seem that a philosophical critique of such a religion would have to take seriously that claim, not necessarily by accepting it but at least by dealing with it.

Many philosophical critiques, however, seem to treat Christianity as if it were a natural religion—i.e., a religion whose real epistemological bases were to be found in arguments, inferences from propositions which were accepted by every sane person, inductions from universally acknowledged facts about the world, and so on. David Hume, it seems to me, is an example of one who takes this approach. He has extensive critiques of arguments for Christianity, or for its theistic underpinnings. But there is little consideration of how revelation might play a role in providing a basis for this faith.

Perhaps this curious feature is not entirely Hume's fault, nor that of other critics who have shared it with him. One can hardly avoid the suspicion that maybe the philosophical critics have treated Christianity as a natural religion because its philosophical friends have often defended it as if it were a natural religion. Perhaps there is a nice chicken-and-egg problem here in the history of philosophy. I don't want to go very far back in that project, but I do want to mention two related conjectures of my own about what may have happened to Hume. Then I will devote the major part of this paper to discussing the substantive issues which are involved in one of those conjectures.

My first conjecture is that Hume may have thought that, whatever Christianity may have been in the beginning, it must *now* be some sort of natural religion. For, he may have reasoned, the people who now believe in the Christian doctrines are not themselves receiving a revelation from God. If their faith is to have any satisfactory basis it must be provided by some sort of natural reasoning. Even if, for example, it is connected with some revelation to ancient prophets, this must be mediated by some argument from testimony. So the right way to treat Christianity, *as it exists now*, is as a natural religion.

This conjectured reasoning which I have ascribed to Hume would find a parallel, I think, in his celebrated treatment of the topic of miracles.[1] It has been noted that Hume's critique there, even if we accept it without question, has nothing at all to say to someone who believes himself to be an eye-witness of a miracle. The critique is directed entirely against a reliance on *testimony* about miracles. But presumably there would be no testimony about miracles if there were not some person who believed, or at least claimed, that his own knowledge of the miracle was based not on testimony but on a more direct experience. Hume, however, seems to ignore such a person.

Here too, Hume may have thought that he was dealing with the actual religious situation of his contemporaries. He says, in fact, that the testimonies about miracles all come to us from remote times, from barbarous countries, and so on. The prodigious events do not seem to happen in our own time and culture. So maybe none of us can do other than to rely on some principle for the evaluation of ancient and uncouth testimony.

We may, however, feel like taking all this with a grain of salt when we also find Hume indicating, a little later in the same section, that he was well acquainted with contemporary testimonies about miraculous happenings. These reports, he tells us, emanated from Paris, they were vouched for by witnesses of the highest integrity, they were tested on the spot by highly respected judges, they were critically scrutinized by well educated enemies of the doctrine with which the miracles were associated, and so on. And so it seems that Hume's own time and culture was not without people whose belief in miracles was not, as they understood it anyway, dependent wholly on testimonial evidence.

That Hume seems both to acknowledge that fact, and also to ignore it (indeed, to deny it flatly) in the course of his argument, is one of the many problems raised by his discussion of this topic. If his treatment of Christianity as a natural religion is parallel to this aspect of his treatment of miracles, then it will generate a similar problem.

My second conjecture about Hume, though not entirely dissimilar from the first, does not attribute to him any belief about a possible difference in the epistemological status of believers in one time and another. For perhaps Hume believed instead that revealed religion—at least if it was to have any chance of epistemic respectability—must *at all times* be a species of natural religion. John Locke, it seems to me, expresses just this view of the matter. He says, "*Reason* is natural *revelation*, whereby the eternal Father of light, and Fountain of all knowledge, communicates to mankind that portion of truth which he has laid within the reach of their natural faculties: *revelation* is natural *reason* enlarged by a new set of discoveries communicated by God immediately, which *reason* vouches the truth of, by the testimony and proofs it gives that they come from God."[2]

This approach makes the legitimate acceptance of a revelation dependent on a prior proof that the alleged revelation came from God. But that is to make a revelation secondary, at best, in the epistemology of the religion. It would not be all that surprising if someone who took this view, or at least took it to represent more-or-less-standard Christian views of the topic, were to conclude that the most deep-going critique of Christianity could largely ignore the idea of revelation, concentrating instead on the extent to which reason can provide proofs of religious matters.

As I said earlier, it is just a conjecture of mine that something like this may lie behind the Humean emphasis on natural religion rather than on revealed religion. However that conjecture may fare, it is the thesis put forward here by Locke whose substance I hope to explore in the remainder of this paper.

Christianity, it seems to me, not only tolerates epistemological enquiry but actually invites it. That is because, in addition to metaphysical claims (such as that God exists and is the crea-

tor of the world) and historical claims (such as that Jesus of
Nazareth rose from the dead), the religion itself includes overtly
epistemological claims. The most striking concept involved
here, and to my mind the most important, is that of *revelation*.
Within the religion the epistemological claims cannot, of
course, be severed from claims of other sorts. It is maintained,
for example, that *historical* personages, such as Moses and Paul,
received divine revelations, and that these revelations occurred
at particular historical times and in specific circumstances. And
it is held that the revealer on these occasions was *God*, the
creator of the world (and the one who sometimes took for
himself the unusually suggestive name "I am"). But while we
cannot completely sever these various claims, we can focus on
one or another aspect, bringing in the others only as necessary.
That is what I hope to do here.

I want, therefore, to explore the concept of *revelation*—more
particularly, divine revelation—and to relate it both to the question of whether believers have (or can have) any reason or basis
for their faith, and to some recent discussions of whether
important parts of Christian belief might be properly basic.

I begin with the notion of basicality.

The idea of a basic belief is derived from a foundationalist
picture of human intellectual life. This picture construes that
life as structurally analogous to a brick building. It may seem
obvious that a brick located forty feet above the ground would
not remain in that position if it were not supported by something. If it is part of a building then it is, of course, supported
by one or more bricks immediately beneath it. These in turn
are supported by lower bricks, and so on. But, since the building is not infinitely tall, this series of bricks and other structural
elements comes somewhere to an end. Somewhere there is a
course of bricks, a concrete foundation, a sleeper beam, or
some such part of the structure, which has no other part of the

structure beneath it. These elements constitute the *foundation* of the building.

The foundationalist construal of a properly structured intellectual life takes beliefs to be analogous to the bricks. Certain beliefs are supported by other beliefs. These may be supported by others, and so on. But the series of beliefs arranged in this way is not infinite. It comes to an end in beliefs which are not supported by any others. These are the *basic* beliefs.

I find the foundationalist picture, as I have described it so far, rather attractive. In the remainder of this paper I will assume this account of our cognitive life, and explore the way in which the notion of a divine revelation may fit into it. But I must emphasize that what I am assuming is the account *as I have given it above.* I do not profess to commit myself, without further investigation, to the additional embellishments which one or another foundationalist philosopher may have added to this picture.

The picture I have sketched, however, is open to an immediate objection. It can be said—correctly, in my opinion—that the version of foundationalism which I have so far described provides no possibility for a critical evaluation of systems of belief. For no pattern of beliefs, no matter how disjointed and no matter how careless of the evidence, could fail to satisfy my account. After all, if a belief is supported by others, then it seems to match one element in that account—it is a derived belief. And if it is not supported by others, then it matches the other element—it is a basic belief. What set of beliefs could possibly fail to pass muster?

I agree that this is an important shortcoming. And it is, of course, just in order to avoid this shortcoming that foundationalist schemes often include a criterion of *proper* basicality. Thus they rule out certain beliefs from proper foundations of a cognitive structure. If those beliefs, then, are not properly derived, they constitute illegitimate elements, and the belief structure which includes them fails to measure up the ideal. My account, which so far lacks such a criterion or any substitute for it, is thus *incomplete*. I hope to remedy that lack, at least in part, as the paper proceeds. I have not done this so far because the additional element which I wish to introduce is not one which I wish to *assume*. To whatever extent I can, I will argue for it.

I can indicate initially the direction which I will follow in that project by calling attention to another element in the building analogy. In an ordinary building the upper courses of bricks rest upon lower courses, until the series ends in the foundations. But it is not as though the foundations rested on nothing at all. Certainly not! The foundations are unique in that they do not rest upon other elements *in the structure*. They do not rest on other parts of the building. But they do rest upon rock, soil, or some other naturally occurring formation. And the stability of the building is only in part a function of the way in which its parts are related to one another—that, is of the degree to which some bricks support others. For in an important way it is also a function of the way in which the foundations are related to something which is not a part of the building at all. It depends on the extent to which the foundations themselves rest on something which is solid. (If this were a sermon, I would refer here to Jesus' parable of the house built on a rock and the house built on sand.)

Does this element of the analogy have a significant epistemological parallel? Later in the paper I hope to argue that it does.

Here, however, we must turn briefly to another question suggested by our picture. Perhaps we understand the support relationship well enough in the case of the bricks. But what is it in the case of beliefs? What is it for a certain belief, p, to support another belief, q, in a certain person's cognitive system? What is the relation which makes p either all or part of that person's evidence for q?

I suppose that our first inclination is to look for the relevant relation in the field of logic. It seems plausible to suppose that p cannot be anyone's evidence for q, unless the truth of p is somehow relevant to the truth of q. And these are just the sort of relations which constitute ordinary deductive and inductive logic. But while it is probably true that some logical relation is necessary for the evidential relation, there is a strong reason for thinking that no such relation is sufficient. For consider the case of a person who has two beliefs, p and q, which have no relevant logical relation to one another, and which are not evidentially supported by any other beliefs held by that person. And now suppose that the person adopts two additional beliefs, $p \supset q$ and $q \supset p$. The resulting quadruple is such that each belief in it is deductively entailed by one or two of the other members of that set. There is nothing wrong with these logical entailments. But it seems highly implausible to suppose that these relations guarantee that these four beliefs are now all evidentially supported in that person's cognitive structure.

For one thing, if these entailments did generate the evidential relation, then that relation (in this case) would be circular. But that seems highly counterintuitive. And further, if one could generate the evidential relation in this way, then no one need be long in the postion of having unsupported beliefs. For it is a trivial matter to apply this technique to any beliefs whatsoever. (And if the original beliefs happened to be true, then the additional beliefs needed to fill out such a set would also be truths.) For these reasons, I conclude that deductive entailment alone cannot be sufficient to generate the evidential relation.

What seems to be missing in this case is any indication that the person holds these beliefs *because* he holds the others. Of course, he might believe $q \supset p$ because he holds p, and he can deduce the former from the latter. In that case it is plausible to say that p does bear the evidential, or supporting, relation to $q \supset p$. But then, though he would indeed believe p, he would not believe it because it is entailed by q and q⊃p, even though he does believe the latter propositions also. It is not easy to say anything positive which will further illuminate the relation which this "because" expresses. There is, however, good reason to think that it cannot be any purely logical relation, or combination of them, for it varies from person to person. Some ancient Greeks, I understand, believed that the earth was spherical because they believed (on the basis of observation) that the hull of a departing ship disappeared before the sail. The latter belief was their evidence for the former. I too believe both of those propositions, but I have never made the relevant observations. I believe the proposition about the earth largely on the basis of authority, and I believe the proposition about the ship partly because it can be inferred from the other one (plus some additional assumptions). So, though I have the same beliefs as the Greeks, the evidential relations between them are largely reversed. Their logical relations, however, are unchanged. I conclude, therefore, that the evidential relation cannot be identical with any set of logical relations.

Perhaps this relation is sui generis or unanalyzable, in the sense that it cannot be resolved, in any illuminating way, into other relations. But even if that is so, perhaps we also have enough grip on this relation (from our own experience of it?) to think about it in the absence of such an analysis. I will proceed on that hope here, continuing to refer to this relation as something with which we have some acquaintance. And I will accept the rather common assumption that this relation is transitive, asymmetric, and irreflexive.

Now, John Locke, as I said earlier, suggested a sort of *scenario* in which revelation seems to play a straightforward epistemological role, readily worked into a foundationalist picture of things.[3] According to this scheme, a person would "first" form the belief that a certain piece of information had been revealed; he might, say, come to believe that the order of events in the creation of the world had been revealed to Moses, who then wrote out an account of what had been revealed to him. This person would then combine this belief with a general principle, apparently endorsed by Locke, to the effect that any-thing which is divinely revealed is certainly true.[4] And so the person would thus come to believe the information itself—in this case, that is, some information about the order of creation.

The general pattern of this scenario, and its logical structure seem to present no special difficulty within the foundationalist picture of things. The final belief is logically entailed by the two beliefs mentioned earlier. Assuming that these two really are the basis on which the final belief is accepted, an assump-tion which I expressed above by using the word "first," it looks as though the final belief finds a place as a derived belief in a straightforward way. And its derivation depends on a belief about revelation. So far, so good.

We can readily recognize, however, that the substance of these beliefs, as distinct from their logical relations, generates a serious (though perhaps not intractable) problem. This is the problem of finding a sufficient basis for accepting the first-mentioned belief, the belief that this information had indeed been revealed to Moses. For if this belief does not itself have a sufficient basis in the cognitive structure in which it appears, it cannot lend satisfactory support to beliefs derived from it, regardless of the strength of the deriving relation. Locke him-self recognizes, I think, that it may be a matter of some diffi-culty to find a satisfactory basis for this belief about revelation, and he must surely be right about that. After all, Moses lived a long time ago, and we may well be at a loss to know how to confirm the claim that he really did stand before a bush which burned without being consumed and heard a heavenly voice speaking to him.

This way of squeezing some cognitive juice out of a revelation will succeed if it is possible to find a satisfactory basis for the belief that the original revelation occurred. While that might be difficult in one or another case, I myself know of no substantial reason for thinking it to be impossible in general. Of course, some people may think that it really is impossible. But that proposition too is one which seems to need some support. In the absence of some persuasive reason for accepting it we may well leave open the question of whether the Lockean scenario can be carried through.

Though I have no interest in denying the applicability of Locke's suggestion to some cases, in this paper I want to try a different revelation scenario. Locke himself distinguishes a reliance on what he calls "traditional revelation" from the case of "immediate and original revelation."[5] In the former case, a person who is not himself the recipient of a revelation relies on a "tradition" which ascribes a revelation to someone else. And it is to this sort of case that Locke applies his scenario. The other sort of case is that of the person who is herself the recipient of a revelation. Locke says little about it, perhaps because he supposed that it had little application to his time or audience. But we have already noted that sometimes he writes as if even the original recipient is in need of "proofs," so that she is not in a markedly better position than later believers. At any rate, it is the case of original revelation with which I will deal here.

If I believe some theological proposition because I believe that it was revealed to Moses, then evidently I do not hold the theology as a basic belief. And it may seem implausible to suppose that I could hold the belief that Moses had a revelation as one of my basic beliefs, or at least that I could properly do so. If we think of Moses himself, however, taking seriously the possibility that he may really have been the recipient of an "immediate" revelation, then perhaps it is not so implausible to suppose that he may have some relevant basic belief about the matter. That is what I want to explore.

Maybe it is worth becoming a little more habituated to just what a basic belief involves. I have a lot of basic beliefs, and many of them are not specially religious. One of my basic beliefs, for example, is that

(1) T-A-B-L-E is the correct or standard spelling of the word "table."

This claim, I have found, sometimes arouses a surprising amount of resistance. It is said, for example, that surely it is possible, even easy, to find evidence in support of (1). And of course it is. But in making the claim that (1) is a basic belief of mine I am not engaging in *hypothetical* epistemology. I am making no claim at all about what might (or might not) have been. I am making a claim about the actual structure of my own cognitive life right now. I do not deny that someone else might have a different cognitive structure, nor that my own might have been different if my intellectural history had been different.

Further, I am not claiming that my belief in (1) is innate, nor that I did not learn the information in (1) in some way or other. In fact, I think it almost certain that I did learn the spelling of this word, possibly from a teacher, more likely just by observing it in books and magazines.

Moreover, I am not claiming that (1) is a very important belief, that it is self-evident, that it is indubitable, that I would never give it up, or anything of the sort. *I am simply claiming that I believe (1), and that I do not believe it because of, or on the basis of, any other beliefs which I hold.* That is what is meant by saying that (1) is a basic belief.

But, someone says, surely you do have other relevant beliefs. You know about dictionaries, and all that, don't you? And of course I do. I have no doubt, for example, that

(2) standard English dictionaries have an entry for the word "table."

And I also believe that

(3) standard dictionaries almost always show the correct or standard spelling for common words such as this one.

These two propositions, however, though they are undoubtedly true, provide *no support at all* for (1). They do not have the relevant logical relation to (1). They do not entail it, and they are irrelevant to its probability. (2) and (3) are general propositions about dictionaries and spellings. They tell us that the dictionaries have, or almost surely have, the correct spelling for this word. But they do not tell us at all what that correct spelling is. They say nothing whatever about that. (1), on the other hand, is a belief about a particular, specified, spelling. Since (2) and (3) say nothing at all about that spelling, or any other, they cannot, as they stand, provide any support at all for (1).

I do, however, have another belief which, in combination with (3), is logically relevant to the truth of (1). I believe, that is, that

(4) Standard dictionaries show T-A-B-L-E as the spelling of the word "table."

And (4) and (3), taken together, are highly relevant to the truth of (1). For (1) is very probable, relative to the combination of (4) and (3).

Nevertheless, (4) and (3) do not, so far as I can tell, constitute any part of *my* reason for believing (1). They might, of course, function in that way for someone else, but in my case they do not. And I have a reason for this latter belief.

My reasons for thinking that (4) and (3) are not my reasons for (1) is that, in my case, the evidential relations are reversed. I believe (4) because I believe (1) and (3), and because I recognize that (4) is highly probable relative to (1) and (3). (4) is thus one of my derived beliefs, and (1) is an essential element in its derivation. If the foundationalist picture is at all correct, therefore, (4) cannot be part of my reason for (1).

There can, of course, be people who have a different reason for (4), and who do not derive it from (1). Someone, for example, may be looking at the relevant page of a dictionary right now, and may be observing the spelling which is given there. Someone else may have recently done so, and may now clearly remember the spelling which she saw there. And so on. But these are not my situations. It is very probable that I have never seen the entry for "table" in any dictionary, and in any case, I now have no memory at all of having done so or of what spelling was there given. So while other people may well have these ways of believing (4) independently of (1), I simply do not.

Similar considerations hold, so far as I can tell, for the other common sorts of reasons which a person might have for (1). No doubt I have often seen this word printed in books, newspapers, etc. No doubt, too, such sources usually have the standard spelling for common words. And I am sure that the great majority of those cases have had the spelling T-A-B-L-E. But *why* am I sure of this last belief? It seems clear to me—about as clear as anything concerning my own intellectual life—that my confidence in this is derived from my antecedent firm belief in (1). It is not, after all, as though I now remembered these many occasions on which I have seen this word correctly spelled. Not at all. Though I am sure I have seen this word almost countless times, I do not now have a clear recollection of even a single such occasion, or of the spelling which appeared there. My situation here, then, is parallel to my situation with respect to the dictionary. Though I certainly have beliefs which are clearly relevant to the truth of (1), the epistemic ordering runs in the opposite directions.

But then (to repeat a question which I mentioned earlier) did I not learn the spelling mentioned in (1)? Yes, I did learn it. Possibly it from a teacher, possibly from a dictionary, and much more probably I learned it just by observing the word in a lot of printed works. Those facts, those incidents in my life, have generated in me a belief in proposition (1). My belief *depends* on such incidents. If there had been no such incidents in my life—if by incredible bad luck almost every printed instance of "table" which I encountered had been misspelled—then very likely I would not have believed (1). But though my belief in (1) depends on such incidents, it is not derived from my *beliefs* about those incidents. For those of my beliefs which are about such incidents, and which have the appropriate logical relation to (1), are themselves derived from (1).

What we have here, of course, is the analogue of the fact that in a building the foundations rest on something, but they do not rest on any other part of the building. My belief in (1) does not spring out of nothing. It is, we might say, *grounded* in something, grounded in specific elements of my experience. But it is not grounded in, or based on, or derived from, other beliefs. More specifically, though it is grounded in elements of my experience, it is not based on my beliefs about that experience. For the most relevant elements of my beliefs about those experiences are themselves derived from my belief in (1). If I did not have *that* belief, then I would have no reason at all for supposing that I had had *those* experiences.

Well, we have had a long excursion into the basicality of a comparatively simple and unimportant belief. Let us return now to the topic of revelation, with the hope that we have been armed with something that will be of use. Let us assume for the moment that some human being—call him "Ishmael"—receives a direct and immediate revelation from God. Let this be a "propositional" revelation. We are assuming, that is, that God communicates some piece of information to Ishmael, something which constitutes a proposition; it is a candidate for belief, and it has a truth value. And assume, too, that Ishmael believes the proposition which God communicates to him. I propose that, in the situation just described, *it is possible that Ishmael's belief in this proposition is both basic and grounded in the divine revelation.* If this is so, then we would have here a revelational scenario different from that which I earlier attributed to Locke. And my guess is that this scenario is more important than his, both for understanding what is claimed for the revelation received by the prophets and apostles and also for understanding the epistemological aspects of the faith of contemporary Christians.

My principal line of argument in favor of the proposition which I have emphasized above turns largely on the structural similarity between the revelational case and my belief in proposition (1). I shall try to sketch out that argument here by raising and answering a number of questions about the revelational case, as I construe it, and about the associated thesis.

In the first place, we are asked to assume that God has revealed something to Ishmael. Must not Ishmael therefore believe that God has revealed something to him? And if so, will he not then believe the revealed proposition *because* of his belief that God is the revealer of it? The second question of this pair does not properly arise here, because the answer to the first one is "no," or more properly, "not necessarily." Of course, Ishmael *might* believe that God was revealing something to him, and then perhaps he would believe the information because of his belief that it was revealed. But I see no reason at all to suppose that every recipient of a divine revelation must believe that God has spoken to him. After all, even President Reagan can speak to someone without that person's having to believe that the president has spoken to him.

Given our scenario, of course, the fact that God has spoken to Ishmael is the true explanation of his having the belief which he does have. But nothing in the scenario guarantees that Ishmael himself knows this explanation. Nothing here guarantees that he even has the concept of *revelation*, or, for that matter, the concept of *God*. So he may not be in a position even to entertain the true explanation, let alone believe it. This is parallel to the fact that I may very well have learned the spelling of "table" before I had learned the concept of *learning*, and thus before I could have properly understood how I had come to that belief.

But if Ishmael did not have the belief that God had revealed that proposition to him, then why would he believe that proposition at all? Would he not have realized that he had no reason for it? Yes, he may have had such a realization. But that need not be a barrier to belief. After all, I realize right now that I have no reason for my belief in the correct spelling of "table," or for a host of other basic beliefs. But I hold these beliefs anyway. To be believed without a reason is the hallmark of a basic belief.

It need not be the case, of course, that Ishmael's belief, even in the absence of a reason, is without an explanation. And the explanation may make essential reference to God. Perhaps, for example, a divine revelation is accompanied by a sense of authority, or by an attractiveness, which is unmatched by a communication from any other source. Perhaps that aura of authority, or the beauty of that attraction, is the thing which has generated Ishmael's belief. Perhaps it is true that if it had not been God who communicated this information to Ishmael, then he would not have believed it. But there is no reason to suppose that Ishmael must know that explanation himself. Maybe that explanation lies within the province of systematic theology, or of philosophy of religion. But Ishmael need have no great competence in these disciplines to be the recipient of a divine revelation.

But perhaps Ishmael, whatever he actually does, *ought not* to accept the substance of this revelation without having a reason for it? One suspects that Locke himself would have opted for this position. At any rate, Locke says, "In any truth that gets not possession of our minds by the irresistable light of self-evidence, or by the force of demonstration, the arguments that gain it access are the vouchers and gauge of its probability to us; and we can receive it for no other, than such as they deliver it to our understandings. Whatsoever credit or authority we give to any proposition, more than it receives from the principles and proofs it supports itself upon, is owing to our inclinations that way, and is so far a derogation from the love of truth, as such."[6] Assuming that the proposition which was revealed to Ishmael was not self-evident, this principle would leave him convicted of having no love for the truth.

The claim that the properly basic beliefs can be restricted to those which are self-evident, or to some similarly constrained set, has recently been criticized at length, mainly on the ground that such claims do not satisfy themselves and are thus self-referentially incoherent.[7] Perhaps this line of criticism is sufficiently familiar to us, and I need not repeat it here. I will content myself for the present with observing that if Locke were correct on this point, then my belief in (1), though it involves no reference to theology or to revelation, would be defective in a similar way. And that seems, to me at least, totally implausible.

We may still, however, feel dissatisfied with this state of affairs. I observed earlier that my initial sketch of the foundationalist picture did not provide for a critique of cognitive structures. Perhaps it is time to fulfill my promise to add to it an element which allows for just such a critical evaluation.

The basis for such an addition has already been suggested. I have distinguished between a belief's being *derived from*, or based on, reasons—i.e. on other beliefs, and its being *grounded on* something other than beliefs—e.g., on some sort of experience. My belief in (4), for example, is derived from by belief in (1) and (3). My belief in (1), on the other hand, though it is not derived from any other belief, is grounded on my long experience with printed English works. And it may well be that basic beliefs, or some classes of them, are legitimate or appropriate only if they are suitably grounded.

What would constitute the suitability of a grounding? I think that I do not know a fully general answer to that question, though it seems plausible to suppose the the suitability of a ground will have something to do with its relation to the truth of the belief which it generates. In any case, even in the absence of a general criterion of suitability we may have confidence in some negative criteria. For example, I mentioned earlier the Lockean assumption that anything which is divinely revealed is certainly true. If we reject this assumption—if we believe instead that divine revelations are usually misleading, deceptive, and false—then it will also be plausible for us to suppose that Ishmael's belief, assumed to be grounded on just such a revelation, is cognitively defective. And if we hold that printed works generally do not have the standard spelling of common English words, then in the same way we will think that my belief in (1) is some way intellectually illegitimate.

But do we in fact have reason to believe that divine revelations are generally unreliable? that they are, for example, less conducive to truth than are standard dictionaries? I, at any rate, do not find in myself any such reason. So I would not have this reason for rejecting the claim that Ishmael's theological belief, grounded in a revelation, was cognitively appropriate.

But surely, someone will say, the crucial question is not that of whether divine revelations are reliable. It is rather the question of whether Ishmael really did have a genuine revelation. Why should we assume that he did? After all, his saying so does not make it so.

I agree that this is the most important question, the deepest one. And certainly Ishmael's saying that he had a revelation would not guarantee that he really had one. (That is one of the reasons I did not propose to assume that Ishmael said that he had a revelation, or even to assume that he so much as had the concept of *revelation*.) And it is certainly true, or so at least it seems to me, that in a real-life case (as distinct from a hypothetical case introduced as a heuristic device) we should not simply assume that someone has had a revelation. It would be equally illegitimate, however, simply to assume that such a person had *not* had a revelation.

I propose, that is, to construe expressions such as "N has not had a revelation," "N's belief has no satisfactory grounding," and similar negative utterances as if they expressed *propositions*. I take them, that is, to have truth values, and to be candidates for belief. If they are elements in someone's belief structure, then they are there either derived or basic. If they are derived they may be more or less well supported by the beliefs from which they are derived. And if they are basic they may or may not be well-grounded.

Now, it is easy to imagine beliefs which are such that if a person had them, then it would be plausible for him also to claim that Ishmael did not have a genuine divine revelation. Some of these beliefs are rather general, such as the belief that there is no God, or that God is incapable of communicating with us, or that God thinks it beneath his dignity to reveal any information, and so on. Other beliefs which will fill this role are more specific, such as the belief that Ishmael is too much of a scoundrel to be the recipient of divine grace, or that the content of the alleged revelation is false, and so on. But the fact that a person has beliefs of this sort does not guarantee that they are true. Whether they really do support the claim that Ishmael did not have a revelation depends on whether they are true and whether they are themselves well supported. If we come upon someone who seriously puts forward reasons such as these, then we can (if we are interested) undertake to investigate them as well as we are able.

A question, however, is not a reason for a belief. "Why should we suppose that Ishmael had a revelation?" is a perfectly good question, fully legitimate. It is not, however, a reason for thinking that Ishmael did not have a revelation. The question has no truth value. It entails nothing, and it makes nothing probable. A person who propounds a question may be doing something very valuable, but he has not, so far forth, produced any reason for any of his beliefs.

Furthermore, beliefs such as "Ishmael had not proved that he had a revelation," or "Mavrodes has not proved that Ishmael had a revelation" are not, as they stand, suitable reasons for believing that Ishmael did not have a revelation. At best they are incomplete. They can function in this way only in conjunction with the claim that if Ishmael had really had a revelation, then he would have proved it (or Mavrodes would have proved it, etc.). To the extent that the latter claims are unsupported, the former assertions, even if plain facts, become irrelevant.

But does this approach not lead to frustration? Will we not end up in a situation in which one person makes a positive assertion for which he can provide no reason, and his opponent counters with a negative assertion for which he, in turn, provides no reason? How is such an impasse to be resolved? Well, in fact some discussions do come to an impasse. (It is not all that uncommon for philosophical discussion to degenerate into even less rewarding quarrels over who has "the burden of proof.") But it is not an a priori truth that they must all suffer this fate. If the interlocuters come upon some principles and assertions which they both accept, then perhaps they will build a resolution on that basis. While their agreement does not guarantee the truth of what they agree upon, they will themselves presumably be satisfied with it. If they have hit upon a truth, whether by revelation or otherwise, then well and good—they will have both satisfaction and truth. And if not? We cannot make humanity infallible by propounding an epistemological principle. For our epistemological conjectures, like all others, run the risk of falsehood.

If some real-life Ishmael propounds a piece of theology it may or may not strike me as important for my own life and thought. If it does, then I can try to evaluate it by any means I find at hand. If at the end of that investigation it seems to be that it is clearly true (or false), then I can accept it (or reject it). And if in the end I find myself still undecided, well then, undecided I am. Now, if Ishmael himself, or someone on his behalf, asserts that this piece of theology was divinely revealed to him, then he does not therby settle the question. He simply adds still another claim to the pot—one which raises essentially the same general sort of problems, and which also is open to the same sorts of resolution. However, this additional claim (like epistemological claims generally) is likely to be less important than the substantive theological information to which it is attached. If God speaks to Ishmael, then that is a great thing for him, a grace of God for his life and faith. But so far forth it is nothing to me. It is not my business generally to determine whether God has spoken to someone else, and it is not surprising that I should often find myself unable to do it.

It might, however, be very important to me that God should speak to *me*, that *I* should have a divine revelation. And there might be some piece of theology whose truth I will be unable to settle if I do not receive that grace. To say that it is a grace, of course, is to say that is is not up to me to secure it—it is up to God to give it. If he does give it to me, then (so far as I can see) the faith which it produces will be well-grounded. And if he does not—or if somehow it is possible for me to reject it—well then, I will not have that word which is the bread of the true life of humanity.

Notes

1. *Inquiry Concerning Human Understanding*, David Hume, sec. x ("Of Miracles").
2. *An Essay Concerning Human Understanding*, John Locke, Ch. xix, sec. 4.

3. Loc. cit., and ch. xviii, sec. 4, 5, and 6.

4. Ibid., ch. xviii, sec. 10.

5. Ibid., ch. xviii, sec. 3.

6. Ibid., ch. xix, sec. 1.

7. See, e.g., Alvin Plantinga, "Is Belief in God Rational?", in C. F Delaney (ed.), *Rationality and Religious Belief* (Notre Dame, Indiana: University of Notre Dame Press, 1979) and his "Reason and Belief in God," in Alvin Plantinga and Nicholas Wolterstorff (eds.), *Faith and Rationality* (Notre Dame, Indiana: University of Notre Dame Press, 1983). I have discussed this pattern of argument in "Self-Referential Incoherence," *American Philosophical Quarterly*, vol. 22, no. 1 (January 1985), pp. 65-72).

David Fate Norton

Hume, Atheism,

And the Autonomy of Morals

> *...when, in my philosophical disquisitions, I deny a provi-*
> *dence and a future state, I undermine not the foundations of*
> *society, but advance principles, which they [the religious phi-*
> *losophers] themselves, upon their own topics, if they argue*
> *consistently, must allow to be solid and satisfactory. David*
> *Hume, (ECHU 13)¹*

According to Descartes, an atheist might in some sense be said to know a simple mathematical proposition (that the three angles of a triangle are equal to two right angles, for example), but this *knowledge* of the atheist "cannot constitute true science, because no knowledge that can be rendered doubtful should be called science," while the atheist, by definition, "cannot be sure that he is not deceived in the things that seem most evident to him . . . doubt . . . may come up, if he examines the matter, or if another suggests it; he can never be safe from it unless he first recognizes the existence of a God."²

If Descartes was concerned about what the atheist could truly know, many of his contemporaries were deeply concerned with what we could know about the atheist. They were concerned, to be more specific, about the morals of the atheist: could an atheist actually be honest, morally upright, a trustworthy and reliable member of society? Could there be, perhaps, a *society* of atheists?

Opinion was, in general, decidedly negative. To be sure Francis Bacon had suggested that atheists were not so wicked as idolaters, and Hugo Grotius said that the basic principles of natural law, derived as they were from the facts of human nature, were sufficiently clear to have effect even if one should maintain so wicked and distasteful a notion as the nonexistence of God: "*That the Laws of Nature would take Place, should we (as we cannot without the most horrid impiety) deny either the Being of GOD, or his Concern in human Business.*"[3]

Even so carefully framed a concession was, however, repudiated with alarm over and over again. Richard Bentley, the first of the Boyle Lecturers, can be seen as typical. The atheist, he wrote,

> allows no Natural Morality, nor any other distinction of Good and Evil, Just and Unjust; than as Human Institution and the modes and fashions of various Countries do denominate them. The most Heroical Actions or detestable Villanies are in the nature of things indifferent to his approbation; if by secrecy they are alike conceal'd from Rewards or Punishments, from Ignominy or Applause.[4]

And he goes on to accuse the atheists of seeking to undo the "Cement of Society" and to reduce man to a state of confusion:

> No community ever was or can be begun or maintain'd, but upon the Basis of Religion. What Government can be imagin'd without Judicial Proceedings? and what methods of Judicature without a Religious Oath; which implies an Omnisicient Being, as conscious of its falshood or truth, and a revenger of Perjury? So that the very nature of an Oath (and therefore of Society also) is subverted by the Atheist; who professeth to acknowledge nothing superiour to himself, no omnipotent observer of the actions of men. For an Atheist to compose a *System* of *Politicks* is . . . absurd and ridiculous . . . .[5]

John Locke had expressed much the same view. In his *Letter concerning Toleration* he argues that "those are not at all to be tolerated who deny the being of a God. Promises, covenants, and oaths, which are the bonds of human society, can have no hold upon an atheist. The taking away of God, though but even in thought, dissolves all."[6] In his even more influential *Essay concerning Human Understanding* Locke went on to argue that "what Duty is, cannot be understood without a Law; nor a Law be known, or supposed without a Law-maker, or without Reward and Punishment," and, although our practical principles are not innate, they do nonetheless presuppose the ideas of "God, of Law, of Obligation, of Punishment, of a Life after this. . . ."[7] In a manuscript work on ethics he wrote:

> The originall & foundation of all Law is dependency. A dependent intelligent being is under the power & direction & dominion of him on whom he depends & must be for the ends appointed him by y^t superior being. If man were independent he could have noe law but his own will noe end but himself. He would be a god to himself, & ye satisfaction of his own will the sole measure & end of all his actions.[8]

Samuel Pufendorf, now too seldom discussed, but perhaps the most influential moralist of this period, repeatedly took the atheists to task.[9] A concern for one's own preservation is, he grants, a fact from which a law of nature of a certain kind, a dictate of reason, may be deduced, but "to give these Dictates of Reason the Force and Authority of Laws, there is a Necessity of supposing that there is a God, and that his wise Providence oversees and governs the whole World, and in a particular Manner the Lives and Affairs of Mankind." The "wicked and absurd Hypothesis" of atheism, should it be accepted, would leave us without moral law, for the "edicts of Reason" cannot "rise so high as to pass into a Condition of Laws; in as much as all Law supposes a superior Power." (P 141–42)

Later in the same work Pufendorf speaks of our "*connate* Obligations," or those that are, "planted, as it were, in our *Being*." The most eminent of these is that

> which lies on all Men with respect to Almighty God, the supream Governor of the World; by Virtue of which we are bound to adore his Majesty, and to obey his Commandments and his Laws. Whoever wholly violates and breaks through this Obligation, stands guilty of the most heinous Charge of *Atheism*; because he

> must at the same time deny either the Existence of God, or his Care
> of human Affairs. Which two Sins, with regard to their moral
> Consequences and Effects, are equivalent to each other; and either
> of them overthrows all Religion, representing it as a frightful
> Mockery, introduced to awe the ignorant Vulgar into some
> Decency and Duty. (P 254)

Pufendorf goes on to denounce even the seemingly
innocuous view of Hobbes, namely, that atheism is the result of
ignorance or imprudence.[10] This view is said to be "most foul
and scandalous," for, although one cannot say that every illite-
rate person is able to form or even to comprehend a "philosophical Demonstration of God's Existence," this gives us no
grounds for doubting or denying his existence. Those with the
effrontery to so doubt are challenged, not only to defend their
atheism, but also to show that it will contribute more to mankind than does the contrary view, theism, or the "Acknowledgment of a Deity." (P 254-55)

The task here set for the atheist, that he provide, in effect, an
entirely new foundation for the concourse of humankind, is
said to be manifestly impossible, if for no other reason than
that one simply cannot rely on the word of any atheist. Those
"who either deny the *Being*, or the *Providence* of God," or those
very like to them, "the Maintainers of the Mortality and
Impunity of human Souls," are beyond our trust, for nothing
can motivate such persons but private interest and advantage.
The promises and covenants of an atheist are no better than
those of any common criminal, while those who do believe in
God have the advantage of motivation that derives from concern about eternal reward or punishment.

> For 'tis impossible, but that Men of these Principles should measure
> all Right and all Justice by their own Profit and Convenience. Into
> the same Herd we may pack all those who practise some Villany or
> Vice for their set Trade and Employment; as Pirates, Thieves,
> Murtherers, Pimps, Courtesans, and other profligate Wretches who
> take Perjury for a Trifle, and make a Jest of sacred *Obligations*. (P
> 276)[11]

Pufendorf's widespread influence in the Protestant univer-
sities of his time was in no small part due to the translations and
annotations of another professor of law, Jean Barbeyrac. Not
content with translating Pufendorf's attack on the atheists, Barbeyrac, by means of copious notes, amplified this attack, and
then turned to the subject again in his own *Historical and Critical
Account of the Science of Morality . . . from the earliest Times down to
the Publication of Pufendorf*. Granted, Barbeyrac sometimes
appears to soften Pufendorf's strictures, as when he cites those
who have argued that atheists are not, really, always so bad as
pirates, pimps, and murderers, while on another occasion he
goes so far as to consider the possibility "that Religion is neither the only, nor principal Basis of Society." (P 276, 142) In
fact, he admits that

> there may be amongst these Atheists, Men of Sense and Philoso-
> phers, who, reflecting that it is better for Men to subject themselves
> to certain Rules of Life, than for every Man to follow his Humours
> only, may observe [these Rules] outwardly, so far as they are
> exempt from such Circumstances, as some great Interest present, or
> some violent Passion forces them upon, such Counsels as are rea-
> sonable, calm and aware of the Consequences.

At the same time, however, Barbeyrac appears to take back
these concessions and simply to second Pufendorf. The "common Sort of ignorant People, and Idiots," he says—those who
comprise "the greatest Part of Society"—are quite unable to
manage such careful reflections. Consequently, to curb "the
Violence of their Passions, and to outweigh Mens private Interests . . . some more obvious Principle, which all the World may
be sensible of, and which may make the deepest Impressions
upon them, must be found out, and that, in a Word, can be no
other than the Fear of a Deity." It is, after all, only an outward
appearance of morality that the atheist can manage: If the
notions of honesty, for example, are cut off from any connection to the "Will of God, the supreme Lawgiver, the Author of
our Being, the Protector of Mankind, and of Society," they
become "meer Chimera's...barren Principles, pure Specula-

tions, incapable of laying a Foundation for good Morality, or to produce solid Virtue," while, Barbeyrac claims, it will simply never occur to the atheist that he should adhere to the principles of morality at the cost of his own desires and interests. (P 142, 160) When all is said and done atheism can lead only to the destruction of society:

> The Notion of a GOD, and of an invisible Judge, who will punish Vice and reward Virtue, are naturally so fast linked together, that the most simple have a Sense of it, notwithstanding their other false superstitious Idea's, as appears from the Example of the Pagans. But, as much as Atheism pleases some Men, as the more pure State, nothing but pernicious Consequences can be drawn from it, tending directly to the greatest Looseness and Debauchery; Consequences which are clear to the Sight of all the World, and can't but bring Destruction to a Society, which is composed of Men endowed with such irreligious Principles. (P 142)

The voice of one person in particular was raised against these seventeenth-century attacks on atheists and atheism: that of Pierre Bayle, the author of *Le Dictionnaire Historique et Critique*, the work later viewed as the arsenal of the Enlightenment. Ironically, although he defended the morality of atheists, Bayle himself was very likely a believing Christian whose fideistic Calvinism was no hindrance to a plainspeaking criticism of cant and hypocrisy.[12]

The event that turned Bayle's attention to the issue of atheism and morality was the comet of 1680. In a world not far in time from pure Ptolemaicism, such a celestial event was thought by many to have special significance, to presage some great terrestrial event or events. Such opinions, Bayle argued, were little more than crude superstitions, and he buttressed his position with an analysis of causal relations that Hume must surely have appreciated. Here, however, we are concerned with the fact that Bayle's effort to overturn the view that comets are omens led him, as he says, to draw "a parallel between Atheism and Paganism" and to enlist "whatever Logic and History" could provide in order to defend his objections to, as it were, astrology. In the sequel this parallel all but eclipsed the original concern.[13]

Bayle's discussion proceeds diffusely, not unlike one of Montaigne's essays. Nevertheless, out of this diffusion there clearly emerges an argument. That argument attempts first to falsify, by an appeal to facts, the claims of the anti-atheists, and then to offer an alternative explanation of human behavior, an explanation that can account for the newly set-out facts. The result is a defense, but not a vindication, of atheism, in so far as it is shown that individual atheists have been (and thus can be) morally upright, and that there could be a society of atheists.

There have been comets, Bayle notes, from time immemorial, and comets that displayed themselves to pagan Europe before the Christian era began. It cannot be, then, that comets are always and necessarily a means by which God seeks to convert atheists to believers. For if comets were always intended to convert atheists to believers, then the pre-Christian comets must have been intended to convert atheists to idolatry, to a pagan religion. That cannot have been the case. Idolatry is as great an evil as is atheism, perhaps even a greater. Idolaters distort and demean the supernatural, picturing their gods as morally weak, even wicked; they revel in profane and heinous practices which they call *sacred* or *religious*; they enmesh themselves in groundless religious superstitions, thereby closing their hearts and minds to the news of the one true Deity. God, who abhors all evil, would not send signs that could lead a generality of mankind into these profaning, shocking sins. God does not use his powers in that way.[14]

For that matter, Bayle goes on, experience of the world shows the fallaciousness of all reasonings intended to show that belief in God corrects the vicious inclinations of mankind. It is widely believed, of course, that man is a reasonable being, determined to desire happiness and avoid misery, and able to control his will by his knowledge of what is the best means for achieving these ends. It is this belief, in fact, that underlies the view that atheism is "the most fearful State" in which a man may be found. For supposing that man is a reasonable agent, and supposing further that individual men are "convinc'd there's a Providence ruling the World, from whom nothing is hid" and who "recompenses the Vertuous with endless Felicity, and the Wicked with everlasting Pains," it seems clearly to follow that the believer acts reasonably and well, while the unbeliever takes "Pleasures as his chief End, and Rule of all his Actions," makes "Jest of what others call Honor and Vertue." and "perjures himself for a trifle." On this account the atheist must be "a Monster infinitely more dangerous than the wild Beasts, Lions, and furious Bulls, of which *Hercules* deliver'd *Greece.*" (B sect. 133)

This view is "all very fine and right," says Bayle, "when one considers things in their Ideas and Metaphysical Abstractions." The difficulty is that the theory bears little resemblance to reality. Visitors from another world having heard about *reasonable* Christians, believing in eternal paradise and torment, would doubtless infer that such a people spend their time in good works, and vie only to see who might excel in charity. The actual facts are immeasurably different, so much so that, were these visitors to "see only one Fortnight's way of the World," they could not but conclude that the practice of Christians is not guided by the light of conscience. Christians employ "their utmost Skill, and all their Passions, to perfect the Art of War"; their soldiers are no less barbaric than any others, as even the story of the crusades makes clear. Christian women are subject and subjected to the same carnal lusts as others; if some are allowed to remain chaste or virtuous, it is only at the expense of those many others who are encouraged in lewdness and prostitution. Christian gentlemen may go to church religiously enough, but out of church they whore and swear, duel and cheat, lie and devise ways "to second their filthy Desires." There is no one with even a little experience of the world who does not know "a thousand Persons firmly persuaded of all the Miracles of Christianity . . . [and] who yet live the most disorderly Lives." If anything at all "be demonstrable in Morality," Bayle says, "I doubt not I have demonstrated" that Christians can be "firmly persuaded of the Truth of their Religion," and yet live a sinful, immoral life, and hence "I conclude that Infidelity is not the source of a Corruption of Manners." That corruption has quite another source. (B sects. 133-48, 159)

Bayle's positive theory, if one may call it that, is a relatively simple one. Christians, he has shown, do not live according to their principles or opinions, nor does any other group act in accordance with its religious beliefs. Generally speaking, human actions are not guided by metaphysical principles, nor even by that most important of all principles, *The Deity exists and concerns himself with human affairs.* How else is one to explain the fact that there is "so prodigious a Diversity of Opinions concerning the manner of serving God, and the Forms of Civil Life," while there is yet on the other hand a no less remarkable uniformity of human behavior? As Bayle puts it, "one finds the same Passions reign eternally in all Countrys, and in all Ages," that "Ambition, Avarice, Envy, Lust, Revenge, and all the Crimes consequent on these Passions" are not merely common, but "rife all the World over," and that "the Jew and Mahometan, Turk and Moor, the Christian and Infidel, Tartar and Indian, the Inhabitants on the Continent and those of the Isles, the Nobleman and the Yeoman, all kinds of Men, who differ in almost all things else, except the general Notion of Humanity . . . so exactly agree" in their actions that one could easily think that they copied from one another. Such uniformity of behavior must spring from "the true Principle of Man's Actions," his natural inclination for pleasure and his desires for particular things, or, in a word, from the passions themselves. Of course, Bayle adds, one must be careful in generalizing about man's motivations, for any rule will be subject to exceptions, but there is nonetheless a rule "which is for the most part true, to wit, *That Man is not determin'd in his Actions by general Notices, or Views of his Understanding, but by the present reigning Passion of his Heart.*" (B sects. 136, 138)

There is, then, no reason to have a special fear of atheists, to suppose either that they must necessarily be more immoral than other men, or that they are less able to participate in society. If it is generally true, "as History and common Life" show, that mankind runs headlong into all kinds of sin, while yet believing this fundamental proposition of religion: "that there's a God who terribly repays the Sinner, and duly rewards the Good," then those that say that belief in this fundamental proposition is a guarantee that the believer will lead a good life are clearly mistaken. Consequently, it is a mistake to suppose that because a man is a believer (either a Christian or an idolater) he will live "a better moral Life than an Atheist." Atheists are motivated by the same principles that motivate idolaters, and both are motivated in exactly the same way that Christians are motivated: by the passions. If every "malicious Inclination results from the Ground of Human Nature, and is fortify'd by the Passions; which rising in the very Mass of our Blood, are infinitely diversify'd according to the different Accidents of Life," then the "Inclination to do ill, belongs no more to a Heart void of the Sense of God, than [to] one possess'd with it." Furthermore, any inclinations we may have to upright behavior—sobriety, good nature, honesty, pity—are owing not to any supposition we may have formed concerning the existence of a Deity, but to our "particular natural Temper and Constitution, fortify'd by Education, by Self-love, Vain-glory, an Instinct of Reason, or such-like Motives," and these "prevail in Atheists as well as others. There's no ground then to maintain, that an Atheist must necessarily be more inordinate than an Idolater." (B sect. 145)

One is not surprised, then, when Bayle writes:

> I make no scruple to declare, wou'd you know my Thoughts of a Commonwealth of Atheists, That as to Manners and Civil Life 'twou'd exactly resemble a Commonwealth of Pagans; 'twill indeed require very severe Laws, and very well executed. But do's not every State require the Same?

That he then goes on to suggest that it is merely because the King of France has given a new force to the "Laws against Bullys and Pickpockets" that there has been a decrease in street crime in Paris makes it clear enough that Bayle thinks a society of atheists would also match a society of Christians, or at least match that of His Most Christian Majesty. There does not happen to be a society of atheists, and perhaps there never has been one. But were there such a society it is probable, Bayle concludes, that it would:

> observe all Civil and Moral Dutys, as other Societys do, provided Crimes were severely punish'd, and Honor and Infamy annex'd to certain Points. As the Ignorance of a first Being, the Creator and Preserver of the World, wou'd not bereave the Members of this Society of a sense of Glory and Contempt, Reward and Punishment, or of all the Passions which reign in the rest of Men, nor wholly extinguish the Light of Reason; one shou'd find Persons among 'em of Integrity in common dealing, some who reliev'd the Poor, oppos'd Violence, were faithful to their Friends, despis'd Injurys, renounc'd sensual Pleasures, did no wrong; prompted to these worthy Actions, either by a love of Praise inseparable from 'em, or a design of gaining Friends and Welwishers in case of a turn in their own Fortune. The Women wou'd set up for Vertue, as an infallible Pledg of the mens Love and Esteem. Crimes indeed of all kinds must happen in such a Society; but not frequenter than in a Society of Idolaters, because all the Principles which prompted the Pagans to Good or Evil, Rewards and Punishments, Glory and Disgrace, Complexion and Custom, take place in a Society of Atheists. (B sect. 172)

Hume met head-on the challenge of the anti-atheists, and in doing so carried the defense of atheism to new levels. But before we turn to Hume some terminological clarifications will give us a better appreciation of this challenge and of Hume's atheistic response.

The first thing to note is that early modern usage of the terms *atheism* and *atheist* were somewhat different, and considerably broader, than current usage appears to be. In the earlier time these terms expressed, as often as not, a kind of general opprobium—they were epithets used to denounce the heterodox as well as the unbeliever, as is made clear by the fact that Erasmus, Luther, Calvin, and several renaissance popes were among those who were said to be atheists and who were denounced for their atheism. Secondly, early modern writers distinguished between *practical* and *speculative* atheists. Practical atheists were generally considered the less dangerous species for they simply, by their profligate behavior, acted as though there were no God ready to judge and to punish their misdeeds. Such callousness was by no means good, but it was thought to be considerably less insidious, less dangerous, than even the most circumspect theorizing of the speculative atheist.[15] Thirdly, we should bear in mind the position reported by Thomas Stanley in his seventeenth-century history of philosophy: the term *atheist*, he says, may be "taken two ways": It may refer to "him who believeth there are no Gods," or to "him who is an enemy to the Gods."[16] It will be seen that on each of these three uses one can be an atheist without making an outright denial of the existence of a god or gods, while on the third use of the term, the class of atheists is seen to include those individuals who are opposed to the gods, or those we might call *a-theists*: individuals who are opposed to the gods or who indicate that they can manage quite well, thank you, without a god or gods.

This third and philosophically significant understanding of atheism is fundamental to the controversy reviewed above. We have seen, of course, that *atheist* and *atheism* were used in highly charged ways, and that it was mainly speculative atheism that concerned Bentley, Pufendorf, Barbeyrac and their contemporaries. Even more importantly, however, we find speculative atheism being given, by our own standards, a broad but reasonably clear definition. A (speculative) atheist is a person who maintains, in one form or another, the truth (or perhaps merely the likelihood) of any one of the following propositions:

1. There is no God, no intelligent first cause of the universe.

2. There is or may be a God, but he takes no interest in the affairs of the universe; there is or may be a Deity, but there is no Divine Providence that guides the affairs of man.

3. Humans have no immortal soul, and hence there are no eternal and divine rewards or punishments; the human soul has, in effect, impunity.

It is to the man who fits this description of the atheist that the anti-atheists, here most fully represented by Pufendorf and Barbeyrac, make their challenge. That challenge in a general form is unambiguously articulated by Pufendorf, while a more specific and rather different sounding challenge (but one that comes to much the same thing) is enunciated by Barbeyrac.

> For in as much as the whole Race of Men in all Ages have constantly held this Persuasion [of God's existence], whoever would attempt to assert the contrary, must of Necessity, not only solidly confute all the Arguments produced on the other side, but also alledge better and more plausible Reasons for his own particular Opinion. And farther, since the Safety and Happiness of Mankind have been hitherto thought to depend chiefly on this Belief, it is requisite, that he likewise prove *Atheism* to contribute more to the Interest and the Good of all Men, than the Acknowledgment of a Deity. (P 254)
>
> It is certain, that *Morality is the Daughter of Religion, that they go hand in hand together; and that the Perfection of the latter, is the Standard of Perfection in the former.* . . . In Fact, the fundamental Principles of Natural Religion, which must be the Basis of all other Religion; are also the most firm, or rather only, Foundation of this Science of Morality.

Without a Deity, *Duty, Obligation, Right,* are no more, to say the Truth, than fine Ideas; which may please the Mind, but can scarce touch the Heart; and which of themselves, cannot impose an indispensible Necessity to act or not to act, in such or such a certain manner. . . . But to give these Ideas their full Force and due measure of Efficacy; to make 'em strong enough to maintain their Ground against Passion and Self-interest; they will require a superiour Being; a Being superiour to us in Power and Might, who has subjected us to a strict Conformity therewith in our Conduct; who has bound us thereto . . . who has put us under an *Obligation,* properly so call'd . . . This Fear of a Deity, who punishes Vice and rewards Virtue, has so great an Efficacy; that, altho' the fundamental Principles of Religion be much darken'd, by the Intermixture of Errour and Superstition; yet if they are not entirely corrupted and destroy'd, it will still continue to actuate, and have a considerable influence. . . . But shou'd you make the finest System in the World, if Religion has not its part in it, it will be little more than (as I may say) a speculative Morality; and you will be found to build on a sandy Foundation. (P *Hist. Account* 14–15)

More than one Hume scholar has argued that Hume's religious position was misunderstood by his contemporary critics and their nineteenth-century successors, a great majority of whom thought Hume a religious sceptic *par excellence,* an atheist.[17] If *atheist* is used in only a strict present-day sense, to refer to a person who explicitly denies the existence of a god or gods, one could conclude that Hume was not an atheist, for we have, so far as I know, no record of such an outright denial. I suggest, however, that such a conclusion is anachronistic and seriously misleading; by the standards of his contemporaries Hume was indeed an atheist. As we have already seen, explicitly denying the existence of the deity was not a necessary qualification of the early modern atheist, while on the other tests of atheism set by the anti-atheists of his time, Hume scores impressively:

    1. Hume clearly, explicitly attacked the notion that there is a deity who takes an interest in human affairs, the

notion, that is, that there is some significant form of divine providence. He argues that the very concept of a miracle is incoherent and, even if that were not so, the evidence in favor of any purported miracle is inadequate to establish that a divine intervention has taken place. Such evidence is not only suspect, but congenitally so. In addition, the world or the universe itself, commonly alleged to bespeak an intelligent, concerned creator, presents us with a mixed bag of evidence, with evil as well as good, so that the argument from design fails for lack of a compelling major premise. If the minor premise is not equally suspect, the very form of this so-called argument is, for it purports to carry us beyond the suggestion that the effects we experience have some cause, to a very different conclusion, namely, that these effects are the consequences of an omniscient, omnipotent, omnibenevolent Creator.[18]

2. Hume allowed to the idea of god only the absolute minimum of content. Assuming that Philo of the *Dialogues* speaks for him, Hume can be so expansive as to say that we should give a "plain, philosophical assent" to "one simple, though somewhat ambiguous, at least undefined proposition, *that the cause or causes of order in the universe probably bear some remote analogy to human intelligence.*" (D 227) In a less expansive mood, and clearly speaking for himself, Hume argued that the origin of the idea of god lies in the ignorance and fear of primitive man and that from this natural beginning we have added and subtracted characteristics extracted from one human source or another, and augmented these by the addition of that most incomprehensible of all philosophical concepts, the infinite.[19] Given the lack of irreducible religious content in even the most sublime form of the idea of the deity, one might suppose that Hume had no real reason to make an outright denial of the existence of a deity or deities.[20]

3. Hume explicitly attacked what he took to be the strongest arguments favoring belief in the immortality of the soul, and he gave a clear and unequivocal testimony of his belief in his own mortality. After reviewing the kinds of arguments available to prove the immortality of the soul, Hume concludes that the matter is quite beyond the range of effective argumentation: "By what arguments or analogies can we prove any state of existence, which no one ever saw, and which no way resembles any that ever was seen? Who will repose such trust in any pretended philosophy, as to admit upon its testimony the reality of so marvellous a scene? Some new species of logic is requisite for that purpose; and some new faculties of the mind, that they may enable us to comprehend that logic."[21] This remark does leave open the possibility that, as an act of faith, Hume nonetheless believed in personal immortality. We can thank James Boswell, however, for closing out that issue by asking Hume, when the latter was obviously on his deathbed, "if it was not possible that there might be a future state." To this question Hume responded by saying that "it was a most unreasonable fancy that he should exist for ever."[22]

There is more. Hume was not content with a quiet, even affable, criticism of theism. He was also an active, aggressive enemy of the gods, an enemy who met the anti-atheistical challenge head-on by arguing that the theists have it precisely backward: Religion does not make morality possible; *religion makes morality impossible*. Wherever it exists—and it defies extermination—religion corrupts morality. There is not space here to review even briefly the lifetime of works in which Hume made this point, but it can be safely said that from the publication of *Essays Moral and Political* in 1741 to the posthumous publication of the *Dialogues concerning Natural Religion* in 1779, no major work by Hume failed to probe critically some aspect of religious belief or religious practice, and more often than not, his attention was drawn to the morally corrupting effects of religion.[23]

The clearest statement of the critical portion of Hume's a-theistical view of morality is found in his *Natural History of Religion* (1757). It was originally intended that this work would appear in a volume entitled *Five Dissertations*, along with, most relevantly for my purposes here, Hume's essays on the immortality of the soul and on suicide. As it happens, however, a prepublication copy of the volume fell into the hands of one of Hume's most outspoken critics, the Rev. (later Bishop) William Warburton, and Hume decided, out of an "excess of prudence," as he later put it, to withdraw the two essays mentioned. At the same time, although perhaps not for the same reason, he modified ever so slightly the *Natural History* itself. This bow to prudence may have avoided a lawsuit, but it scarcely satisfied Warburton, who wrote to Andrew Millar pointing out to him that Hume's revisions and excisions changed not the fact that the author "is establishing atheism" and that Millar had published a book designed "to establish *naturalism*, a species of atheism, instead of religion."[24]

About the *naturalism* of the *Natural History of Religion* Warburton is entirely correct. The work is an unrelenting, naturalistic account of religious phenomena and, consequently, a sustained attack on theism and on Christianity itself. Granted, Hume opens the work by distinguishing between the foundation of religion in reason and its foundation in human nature, and by claiming that

> The whole frame of nature bespeaks an intelligent author; and no rational enquirer can, after serious reflection, suspend his belief a moment with regard to the primary principles of genuine Theism and Religion.

But, by the time he has finished his consideration of the other question, that "concerning the origin of religion in human nature," we see that these "primary principles" are rather different from those we might have expected. (NHR I; W 4:309)

Hume begins by noting that there apparently have been some nations or peoples who "entertained no sentiments of Religion." Among those who do have such sentiments there are very great differences of opinion: "no two nations, and scarce any two men, have ever agreed precisely in the same [religious] sentiments." Given these facts, it cannot be said that our religious conceptions are the effect of any "original instinct or primary impression of nature." They are not on a par with "self-love, affection between the sexes, love of progeny, gratitude, resentment," for the effects of these have been found to be "absolutely universal in all nations and ages," and each such underlying instinct is seen to have "always a precise determinate object, which it inflexibly pursues." Our basic religious principles must, then, be secondary principles, or principles of a sort that "may easily be perverted" or "altogether prevented" by various accidents and causes. It is the secondary principles that give rise to religious belief, and the accidents or causes that shape this belief, that are the subject of Hume's ensuing discussion. (NHR I; W 4:309-10)

This discussion is a major contribution to the debate about atheism and morality, a contribution that goes well beyond Bayle's claim that there could be a society of atheists and that such a society could be at least as moral as a society of pagans, or, as we read between the lines, Christians. The central teaching of the *Natural History of Religion* is that theism, including unmistakably popular Christian versions of theism, serves to corrupt morals and society. The anti-atheist challenge is: prove that atheists can be as upright as theists. Hume responds with an aggressive riposte: atheists, as they are not blinded by superstition, are not encouraged in bigotry, are not led to practice the monkish virtues—atheists are easily the moral superiors of theists.

Polytheism or idolatry, Hume says, "was, and necessarily must have been, the first and most ancient religion of mankind." The historical facts support this contention, and so does the logic of development. When we consider our most ancient records of man, we see that he was then a polytheist. Can we suppose that in still more ancient times that was not the case, that while mankind was "ignorant and barbarous" the truth was discovered, only to be lost as learning increased? Such a supposition is not only improbable in itself, but it contradicts experience of "the principles and opinions" of presently existing people. The uncivilized tribes of America, Asia, Africa are all idolaters. We can as easily imagine that men lived in palaces before they occupied huts as to believe that they first conceived of the Deity as "a pure spirit, omniscient, omnipotent, and omnipresent," before they took him to be "a powerful, though limited being, with human passions and appetites, limbs and organs." The human mind simply does not work in that way, but, rather, rises gradually from the inferior to the superior. (NHR I; W 4:310-11)

But what led men to frame any kind of religious hypothesis? It was not, one can be sure, the contemplation of the works of nature as constituting a smoothly functioning whole in which every part is well adjusted to contribute toward the completion of a well-designed plan. Such a consideration would have made theism, not polytheism, the first religion of mankind, for seeing the universe as a whole would naturally lead one to suppose it the work of a single artificer. Nor did primitive man see nature as such a whole. On the contrary, nature, if it was noticed at all, was seen as broken and mysterious; the events of life and nature were viewed with puzzlement, with ignorance and with, most of all, fear. The seemingly inexplicable events of nature came to be understood as the province of some petty or awesome power(s), presumably intelligent, and able to be propitiated. We see, then, that the principles of human nature on which religion is founded are the

> ordinary affections of human life; the anxious concern for happiness, the dread of future misery, the terror of death, the thirst of revenge, the appetite for food and other necessaries. Agitated by hopes and fears of this nature, especially the latter, men scrutinize, with a trembling curiosity, the course of future causes, and examine the various and contrary events of human life. And in this disordered scene, with eyes still more disordered and astonished, they see the first obscure traces of divinity. (NHR II; W 4:313-16)

Man, Hume goes on, is perpetually suspended between "life and death, health and sickness, plenty and want," conditions that are "distributed amongst the human species by secret and unknown causes." In this condition we focus on these unknown causes, and while they are the object of our hopes and fears, while our passions keep us in a state of constant alarm, our imagination forms for us ideas of those powers on which we seem to depend. Were we able at this point to dissect each part of nature as the best natural philosophy can now do, we would no doubt find that these unknown and awesome causes are merely the "particular fabric and structure" of ourselves or nature. Lacking that hard-won skill, the ignorant multitude muddles on, and consistent with a "universal tendency" of our nature, they personify these causes. It is not only in the moon or clouds that mankind find faces or other human shapes. The secret and unknown causes that we fear come in for the same treatment; they are given "thought and reason and passion, and sometimes even the limbs and figures of men." (NHR III; W 4:316-17)[25]

From fear, polytheism; from fear and polytheism, theism. It was the disorder of their circumstances that led primitive men to a belief in deities, and it is disorder that leads the current multitude to believe in a supreme and particular providence. Not even the masses of modern Europe are brought to their religious opinions by any process of rational argument. They, like their ancestors, base these opinions upon "irrational and superstitious principles," and it is precisely these principles that transform polytheism into theism. (NHR VI; W 4:328-30)

An idolatrous people, although they recognize several deities, will often, nonetheless, see one of these as superior to the rest. When this happens, the worship of this apparently superior deity will take exaggerated and flattering forms, and

> as men's fears or distresses become more urgent, they still invent new strains of adulation; and even he who outdoes his predecessor in swelling up the titles of his divinity, is sure to be outdone by his successor in newer and more pompous epithets of praise. Thus they proceed; till at last they arrive at infinity itself. . . .

Of course it is unlikely that the masses understand the increasingly sublime attributes that are ascribed to the supreme deity, but "thinking it safest to comply with the higher encomiums, they endeavour, by an affected ravishment and devotion, to ingratiate themselves with him." By this entirely natural and unmysterious process, then, does the fundamental belief of the theist arise. (NHR VI, VII; W 4:330-33)

But, although the origin of theism can be traced to polytheism, and though either of these two forms of religion may gradually be transformed into the other, it does not follow that there are no genuinely important differences between theism and polytheism. Sections IX-XII of the *Natural History* offer a comparison of polytheism and monotheism with regard to persecution and toleration, courage or abasement, reason or absurdity, and doubt or conviction.

Polytheism, Hume argues, has the disadvantage of appearing so flexible in its tenets that there is no practice or opinion that it could not support; on the other hand it has the advantage that it is, by its very nature, highly tolerant of diversity. Theism has the contrary advantages and disadvantages, but appears to come off a poor second just because of its natural tendency toward intolerance. It should set before mankind "the most illustrious example, as well as the most commanding motives, of justice and benevolence." It is more likely to set a bad example as its sects "fall naturally into animosity, and mutually discharge on each other that sacred zeal and rancour, the most furious and implacable of all human passions."[26] Theism, because it represents the deity as infinitely superior to mankind and is at the same time joined with "superstitious terrors," is likely "to sink the human mind into the lowest submission and abasement, and to represent the monkish virtues of mortification, penance, humility, and passive suffering, as the only qualities which are acceptable" to the Deity. The deities of polytheism, in contrast, are so little different from ourselves that we are offered the prospect of emulating, even rivalling, them, and consequently "activity, spirit, courage, magnanimity, love of liberty, and, all the virtues" that make a people greater are encouraged. (NHR IX; W 4:336-39)

A fair examination of ancient polytheism, Hume goes on, will reveal that this religion is not so absurd as one might at first suppose. It is only the view that, whatever powers or principles formed the world that we inhabit, these powers also produced "a species of intelligent creatures of more refined substance and greater authority than the rest." Indeed, "the whole mythological system is so natural" that it seems more than likely to have been instantiated somewhere in the universe. Theism, in contrast, seems at first so reasonable that philosophy itself is joined with theology—with disastrous consequences. For philosophy finds herself

> very unequally yoked with her new associate; and instead of regulating each principle, as they advance together, she is at every turn perverted to serve the purposes of superstition . . . one may safely affirm, that all popular theology, especially the scholastic, has a kind of appetite for absurdity and contradiction. If that theology went not beyond reason and common sense, her doctrines would appear too easy and familiar. Amazement must of necessity be raised: Mystery affected: Darkness and obscurity sought after: And a foundation of merit afforded to the devout votaries, who desire an opportunity of subduing their rebellious reason, by the belief of the most unintelligible sophisms. (NHR XI; W 4:341-42)[27]

On each point of comparison, then, Hume finds polytheism

superior to monotheism. In view of this finding, it is all the more significant that he has already argued that polytheism is, when all is said and done, *a form of atheism*. There is, Hume had argued, only a relatively small and insignificant difference between the atheist who says there is no "invisible, intelligent power in the world," and the polytheist who posits a bevy of deities practically indistinguishable from such quasi-material beings as elves and fairies. In contrast, the difference between the polytheist and the genuine theist is enormous, despite the fact that our language leads us to treat the two positions as similar. It is "a fallacy," Hume writes, "merely from the casual resemblance of names, without any conformity of meaning, to rank such opposite opinions under the same denomination." And he goes on to conclude that

> These pretended religionists [the polytheists] are really a kind of superstitious atheists, and acknowledge no being, that corresponds to our idea of a deity. No first principle of mind or thought: No supreme government and administration: No divine contrivance or intention in the fabric of the world. (NHR IV; W 4:320)[28]

In short, Hume finds that so far as several crucial social virtues are concerned, polytheism is demonstrably superior to monotheism, while in general the morals of polytheists are necessarily less corrupt than those of the theists.[29] But if polytheism is morally superior to monotheism, and yet polytheism and atheism are essentially one and the same, then one can equally well conclude that atheism is morally superior to monotheism. Whether one agrees or disagrees with Hume's conclusion, one must grant that he has challenged head-on the claim that religion, and especially theism, provides the foundation of morality and the cement of society.[30]

As represented by Pufendorf and Barbeyrac, the anti-atheists can be seen to have presented four principal challenges to the atheist:

    1. Given the nearly perfect universality of belief in a

providential deity, the atheist is challenged to confute the arguments that support this belief.

2. The atheist is then challenged to show that his own position is supported by "better and more plausible" arguments than is the theistic position he has confuted.

3. Given the nearly perfect universality of the opinion that religious belief is the cement of society, the atheist is challenged to show that atheism contributes "more to the Interest and Good of all Men, than [does] the Acknowledgment of a Deity."

4. The atheist is then challenged to show that there can be an effective, practical morality that is independent of religious belief.

The greater part of Hume's response to this four-part challenge is well-known. None of his philosophical writings is more familiar than those in which he attempted to overturn the arguments purporting to prove the existence of a providential deity. These same arguments gave Hume grounds for claiming that his sceptical position is in fact more plausible than that of the theists, while the *Natural History of Religion* presents his thoroughly naturalistic candidate for the most plausible and compelling account of the origin of religion. And as we have just seen, Hume set out to rebut the theists' claim that religious belief is the cement of society. Religion, Hume argues, is in fact a grave danger to society.

It comes as no surprise, then, to find Hume meeting the fourth of the anti-atheists' challenges. He did so by developing a "system of morals"[31] that derives both moral distinctions and moral motivation from an entirely secular foundation, and that at the same time offers arguments and analyses which, if correct, entirely overturn the fundamental assumptions of those theistic moralists who claim that morality is founded on certain divine commands.

The *divine command theory* of morality presupposes the truth of a number of claims.[32] Those who believe that the only satisfactory account of morality is one that traces its origins to divine commands must also believe that there is a being who, by virtue of (among other things) creating mankind, or controlling the destiny of mankind, is clearly superior to mankind. This superior or supreme being must also be a morally superior being—a being whose every activity is necessarily virtuous.[33] Also, he must be known to take an interest in the affairs and behavior of mankind, and he must demonstrate this interest in human affairs by establishing and promulgating rules or laws (divine commands) that are intended to direct the behavior of rational beings and especially to direct the behavior of individual members of the human race. On the other hand, the creatures whose behavior is to be directed by these commands must be rational beings capable of understanding the commands given them.

In addition, the divine command theory presupposes the truth of at least three other fundamental propositions:

A. Inferior and dependent individuals owe an allegiance to the superior being on whom they depend.

B. Virtue, at least for inferior individuals, consists in conforming one's behavior to rules or laws, while the supreme being rewards those who conform to the divine commands, and punishes those who do not; these rewards and punishments include those administered in an eternal extension of this life.

C. Without the sanctions provided by the fear of eternal punishment or the hope of eternal reward, one can only *understand* a divine command; it is the sanctions, and especially that of fear, that give one the required *desire* to conform one's actions to the command.

Hume's moral theory, especially that of the *Treatise*, is a concerted attack on these fundamental presuppositions.[34] The anti-atheists challenged the atheist to show that there can be an effective, practical morality independent of religious belief. In the most general terms, Hume's response to this challenge may be understood as a modified *tu quoque* argument: Pufendorf and Barbeyrac claim that the atheistic moralist can at best account for no more than the occurrence of barren, merely speculative moral concepts. Hume in response argues that the anti-atheists' theory of morals is a patchwork of superstition and authority that fails of even so meagre an accomplishment as the one mentioned. The anti-atheists themselves fail to account for even the bare attainment of such basic moral concepts as *duty, obligation, allegiance, justice,* or *property,* nor, on their principles, could they ever give such an account. Furthermore, they have completely misunderstood both the nature and foundations of morality, and they have mistakenly conflated acting virtuously, or the acquisition of moral merit, with devotional acts, or the acquisition of religious merit.

Let me begin with the last of these suggestions. Here again we can draw on the *Natural History of Religion* and Hume's suggestions about the foundation of religious practice in human nature.

Suppose, Hume says, someone founded a popular religion[35] in which it were "expressly declared" that nothing but virtuous behaviour could gain the approbation of the deity, and even that this religion were served by an order of priests or clerics themselves entirely satisfied to do nothing more than to teach this opinion through daily sermons. So "inveterate are the people's prejudices," he continues, "that, for want of some other superstition, they would make the very attendance on these sermons the essentials of religion," thus substituting certain ritualistic acts for those of genuine virtue. The difficulty is, it seems, that men simply cannot bring themselves to accept that the best means of serving the deity is "by promoting the happiness of his creatures." On the contrary, because of the terrors with which they are haunted, men "seek the divine favor, not by virtue and good morals, which alone can be acceptable to a perfect being, but either by frivolous observances, by intemperate zeal, by rapturous extasies, or by the belief of mysterious and absurd opinions." That is, religion leads mankind to eschew the practice of virtue, and in its stead take up one or another practice "which either serves to no purpose in life, or offers the strongest violence to [man's] natural inclinations." Just because the practice is useless it is thought to be the "more purely religious." What, after all, could be a surer proof of devotion than to perform austere and bizarre acts that can have no purpose other than the expression of this very devotion.

Two features of Hume's view emerge from these remarks. First, the *practice of religion* and the *practice of virtue* run along paths not merely separate but entirely divergent. Religious acts are motivated out of self-interest, and for that very reason cannot be acts of virtue. Virtuous acts are those done out of regard for the interests of others. But a man who courts divine favor in order to secure "protection and safety in this world, and eternal happiness in the next," is not virtuous, but selfish. In this regard, the divine command theory, as Shaftesbury and Hutcheson had already noticed, is no significant improvement on the selfish theory Hume attributes to Thomas Hobbes.[36] The practice of religion does itself lead men to neglect, even to repudiate, the practice of virtue. Furthermore, in his concern to distinguish himself before his deity, in his concern to focus the divine attention upon himself, the religious man far too often succumbs to the temptation to commit what are nothing less than immoral acts:

> the greatest crimes have been found, in many instances, [to be] compatible with a superstitious piety and devotion: Hence, it is justly regarded as unsafe to draw any certain inference in favour of a man's morals, from the fervour or strictness of his religious exercises, even though he himself believe them sincere. (NHR XIV; W 4:357-59)[37]

These general considerations can serve as background to a necessarily brief sketch of Hume's responses to each of the three presuppositions, A, B, and C.

    C. Without the sanctions provided by the fear of eternal punishment or the hope of eternal reward, one can only *understand* a divine command; it is the sanctions, and especially that of fear, that give one the required *desire* to conform one's actions to the command.

Just above I noted that Hume rejects the claim that fear may be the motive to virtue. This can be amplified in at least two ways. First, Hume rejects a further suggestion of the divine command theory, namely, the claim that we are motivated only by self-interest. In this respect, Hume's criticisms of Hobbes, Locke, and Mandeville serve a double role, as does his own (so he believed) fuller and more accurate account of human nature.[38] The overall effect is to show that fear is far from being the only passion capable of motivating us to action. That is, Hume surveys human nature and human behavior and concludes that we are in fact motivated by a number of passions, including a limited but entirely natural (instinctive, uninstructed) generosity. Consequently, there is no reason to suppose that it is only by adding fear to the mixture that men can be motivated to keep rules or (what is *not* the same thing) to act virtuously. Even if, *contrary to fact,* virtue could be motivated by fear, it would not *necessarily* be motivated by fear. Men are motivated by several passions other than fear, and consequently morality need not be supposed to be dependent upon whatever it is that is said to be attained—motivation or sanction—by positing a divine and threatening lawgiver.[39]

    Secondly, if Hume's general account of the relationship between virtue and motivation is correct, the presupposition of the theist cannot be true. According to Hume, we assign moral blame to a person for not performing an action because we suppose that an individual in the circumstances this person was in "shou'd be influenc'd by the proper motive of that action." If, however, we then find that this proper motive was in fact present and operating, but that its influence was prevented "by some circumstances unknown to us," we withdraw our ascription of blame, and may even assign moral praise. This fact indicates, he goes on, that "all virtuous actions derive their merit only from virtuous motives, and are consider'd merely as signs of those motives." And from this principle he concludes further that the virtuous motive from which an action derives its moral merit "can never be a regard to the virtue of that action." The action does not *become* virtuous (more accurately: the action cannot rightly be *called virtuous*) until it is desired for some reason that itself causes the action to be called virtuous in the first place. This other reason "must be some other natural motive or principle," and this other motive or principle, Hume goes on to argue, is the desire to benefit others. Still other motives may well be reasonable, even natural, but no other motives can give rise to *virtue*. (T 477-78)[40]

This theory of the origin of virtue in motivation will be relevant again below, but for the present it is clear that it runs directly counter to any suggestion that acts motivated by either fear of punishment or hope of reward can ever be virtuous acts; the only acts attaining moral merit are those motivated by a desire to benefit others.

> B. Virtue, at least for inferior individuals, consists in conforming one's behavior to rules or laws, while the supreme being rewards those who are virtuous (those, that is, who conform their behavior to the divine commands), and punishes those (the wicked) who do not; these rewards and punishments include those administered in an eternal extension of this life.

About this claim Hume is dubious for a number of reasons, not the least being his doubts about the immortality of the soul and the existence of that other world in which such rewards and punishments are meted out. But his objections run beyond a mere freethinker's doubts about eternal life. As we have seen that he finds all attempts to found morality on self-interest to be inadequate, it is obvious that he must consider all talk of eternal rewards and punishments quite beside the point of morality. It is possible that there are such rewards and punishments, but they cannot possibly be incentives to *virtue*, nor, on the other hand, can the performance of virtuous acts be of any religious significance. It is not a matter of virtue being its own reward. Hume appears to reject even so austere a prudentialism. It is, rather, that to fulfill a moral obligation is simply to do what one ought to do: "virtuous conduct is deemed no more than what we owe to society and to ourselves."[41]

Furthermore, we lack entirely the grounds for extending our moral concepts to higher beings. Hume told Hutcheson that he had revised Book III of his *Treatise* in an effort to remove all those passages which might give offense to the religious. But despite this further round of prudential revision and the fact that Hume appears to direct his criticism merely at those now known as moral rationalists, the opening section of Book III is clearly apposite to the point under discussion.

Those who maintain an abstract rational difference between moral good and evil, Hume writes, suppose not only that these relations are eternal and immutable but also that their effects must necessarily be always the same and thus that they "have no less, or rather a greater, influence in directing the will of the deity, than in governing the rational and virtuous of our own species." But, he goes on, it is one thing to know virtue, and quite another to conform the will to it. These are distinct particulars. Consequently, in order to prove "that the measures of right and wrong are eternal laws, *obligatory* on every rational mind," one would have to prove that the pretended connection between these allegedly eternal relations and the will is an absolutely invariable connection between a particular cause and a particular effect and is "so necessary, that in every well-disposed mind, it must take place and have its influence." No such proof is possible:

> I have already prov'd, that even in human nature no relation can ever alone produce any action; besides this, I say, it has been shewn, in treating of the understanding, that there is no connexion of cause

and effect, such as this is suppos'd to be, which is discoverable otherwise than by experience, and of which we can pretend to have any security by the simple consideration of the objects. All beings in the universe, consider'd in themselves, appear entirely loose and independent of each other. 'Tis only by experience we learn their influence and connexion; and this influence we ought never to extend beyond experience. . . . we cannot prove *a priori,* that these relations, if they really existed and were perceiv'd, wou'd be universally forcible and obligatory. (T 465-66)

In less elaborate terms, Hume is arguing that our knowledge in the domain of morals is subject to the very limitations that mark the rest of our knowledge. No matter what our subject, we are unable to go beyond experience. Furthermore, just as our experience in natural philosophy and (as we now might say) philosophy of mind or psychology fails to provide knowledge of a deity whose operations solve metaphysical or epistemological problems, so does it fail in morals. Efforts to found morality and obligation on eternal relations deriving from the deity are bound to fail because, as morality is a practical affair involving matters of fact (agents, actions, situations, assessments), the relations between these components are, like all such factual relations, contingent. It appears, then, that morality must be a purely human affair. It is concerned with human actions in the present sphere, it rests on human nature, and it is dependent upon human experience alone. As Hume expressed his general view in a letter: "Morality ... regards only human Nature & human Life."[42]

A. Inferior and dependent individuals owe an allegiance to the superior being on whom they depend.

Hume's objections to this presupposition rest on fundamental and complex components of his system, and hence are difficult to state briefly. Building on the discussion just completed, one could say that, according to Hume, the theist claims to *trace* moral obligation to the command of the deity, but what he in fact does is to *project* onto a putative deity principles and precepts of purely human derivation and application. These he would then have us suppose to be derived from the deity, but in point of fact, so far as Hume is concerned, the theist has salted an otherwise empty mine.

Hume has no interest in doubting or denying that there are obligations such as those we are put in mind of by the term *allegiance*. He even grants that individuals who are especially aided by other individuals owe a debt of gratitude to those who have given the aid, and he suggests that a form of ingratitude, patricide, is the most vicious of all crimes. But allegiance itself, he argues, arises not from the foundation of a dependent relationship. It arises, rather, from private interest controlled by private interest itself, and then turned by purely human interventions into a mundane and secular, but genuine, social virtue. A *moralist* who concerns himself with a putative allegiance to the deity is pursuing a pointless and potentially dangerous speculation that necessarily carries him quite beyond the moral domain.

In somewhat more detail: Hume objects to certain moral theories because they presuppose precisely those fundamental moral concepts whose presence and significance need to be explained, and he goes on to offer the needed explanation.[43] The explanation that he gives, assuming it is correct, reveals that the divine command theory is entirely mistaken in its account of the nature and origin of allegiance, justice, and other such virtues.

Hume distinguishes between *natural* and *artificial* virtues. The former are those qualities (for example: beneficence, generosity, clemency, temperance, frugality, enterprise, greatness of mind) that, like all virtues, "acquire our approbation, because of their tendency to the good of mankind" but are distinguished from other virtues insofar as they are the result of some natural passion or fundamental propensity of human nature itself. In addition, the good that the natural virtues produce "arises from every single act" of this sort. In contrast, although the artifical virtues (for example: justice, promise-keeping, allegiance, chastity), can also be traced, ultimately, to human nature, they are the result of thought, reflection, or contrivance—of human artifice—and are further distinguished by the fact that "a single act of justice [for example], consider'd in itself, may often be contrary to the public good." Where the artificial virtues are concerned, it is "only the concurrence of mankind, in a general scheme or system of action," and the effort to maintain this system at full strength, which in such a case contributes to the good of mankind. (T 578-79)[44]

Justice is the paradigm artificial virtue on Hume's account. Briefly stated, it is Hume's view that, while justice is in fact a full-fledged virtue—acts of justice are acts done for the good of mankind—justice has its foundation in another natural human propensity, our pronounced tendency to pursue or protect our private interests, and also in the fact that certain desirable goods are in relatively short supply. Treating this theory as a historical claim, we can say that when this situation is first comprehended—at a time before justice has become a virtue—individual humans realize that their private or individual interests will best be served by the kind of cooperation that allows each individual to retain control over those goods which he or she has obtained. Hume traces the beginnings of such cooperation to the natural attraction between the sexes, and the consequent development of the family, and thus to human nature itself, but our principal concern here is not with beginnings but with development and transformation. How does one's private interest in retaining the goods one controls contribute to the development of a virtue that cannot be, on Hume's theory, performed out of private interest? Or how, we might ask, are we able to transform one and the same act from an act of proto-justice into a genuine act of justice?

Given that Hume insists that it is a difference of motive that distinguishes acts of proto-virtue from acts of genuine virtue, he must suppose that we are able to change our motivation so that we seek for the good of others that which we previously sought only out of private interests.[45] But granting this, the question returns in another form: What enables us to uphold, say, a system of rules for the transference of property not merely out of the self-interest that gave rise to this system but out of a concern for the good of others, including the good of remote and even unknown persons?

The answer lies in the operation of sympathy, or in the ability of humans to communicate feelings and sentiments from one to another and thus to share ends or aims. Because of this ability I am able to discover that just as I approve of those acts of others that enable me to retain control of my goods, so do others approve of those acts of mine that enable them to retain control of their goods. It then happens that individuals are sometimes motivated to uphold this system of rules simply because such an action benefits and pleases those other individuals who are aware of it. In short, by the operation of sympathy men sense that an act of proto-justice benefits others, and even mankind in general. Consequently, at some point (very early) in the history of mankind one or more individuals was motivated to perform an act of proto-justice, but for a new and qualitatively different reason: in order to bring about the good of others. At that moment, that individual or set of individuals performed not an act or acts of proto-justice, but a virtuous act or acts, and the virtue of justice came into being.

Hume offers the same general account of each of the artificial virtues. Allegiance begins as proto-allegiance, or as an acceptance of government for reasons of self-interest. It cannot be traced to a divine command, nor even to the superiority of a supreme being. On the contrary, allegiance, or the moral duty of submission to government, arises first from the recognition that in certain circumstances one's interests require that there be a civil government capable of protecting those interests. In those circumstances, men "naturally assemble together . . . chuse magistrates, determine their power, and *promise* them obedience," the convention of promise-keeping already having been established as a part of the fundamentals of justice. (T 541) In the course of time, again because of the operation of sympathy, those who are governed begin to see that submission to the government is in the public interest. Because, as Hume puts it, we see that in large societies the execution of justice—the carrying out of certain activities which benefit mankind in general—is "impossible, without submission to government," we first establish a magistrate, and then later give him our allegiance simply because we want to foster this general benefit. (T 546) As soon as that happens the *virtue* of allegiance arises. Allegiance is merely a humanly created, "factitious" duty of obedience, a duty whose "sole foundation," he says, "is the *advantage*, which it procures to society, by preserving peace and order among mankind." (ECPM 205)[46]

Of central importance in the present context, however, is the fact that for Hume allegiance is limited by self-interest, which is to say that our obligation to the magistrate/monarch is not absolute. Citizens owe the magistrate allegiance, but they are not merely his *creatures* or his property, over which he has an absolute authority or right. And because our conceptions of allegiance and obligation derive from this secular context and are informed and controlled by it, there can be no ground for supposing that our allegiance to the deity must be of a different, unmitigated sort, especially as there is inadequate evidence for supposing the deity has been significantly concerned with the formation and operation of the universe.[47]

Hume is known, justifiably, as a skeptic, and especially as a *religious* skeptic. He was not content, however, to establish himself as a mere scoffer, or articulate village atheist, not even to the world at large. But he expressed his dissatisfaction with the role religion had played in human life—with the two hundred years of religious strife that followed upon the Protestant Reformation; with the effects of the more unified Christian church of the pre-Reformation period; with religion wherever he found it in his extensive researches into human history. One of his interlocutors (the Epicurean of the first *Enquiry*) is made to complain about those who use the religious hypothesis as the basis for concluding that this life is "merely a passage to something farther; a porch, which leads to a greater, and vastly different building; a prologue, which serves only to introduce the piece, and give it more grace and propriety." The same interlocutor then goes on to insist that inferring from the course of nature to a "particular intelligent cause" of order is "both uncertain and useless." Uncertain because "the subject lies entirely beyond the reach of human experience"; useless because we can never "return back from the cause with any new inference, or . . . establish any new principles of conduct and behavior." (ECHU 141–42) Granted, in this particular context Hume continues the conversation by doubting whether or not what *ought* to be the case (that life be free of the influence of "religious doctrines and reasonings") actually *is or can be* the case, and he even suggests that, while religious views are ill-founded, they do have a beneficial effect on society for they help to restrain men's passions.

But Hume did not leave it at that. The bulk of his writings suggest that his view of the matter is essentially that of the Epicurean: morality ought to be free of the influence of religion and religious belief and is in fact built on an entirely different foundation. Thus while Hume is a religious sceptic and a sceptic about religiously based moral systems, he is not, and did not conceive himself to be, a moral sceptic. He is, rather, a humanist: he attempts to show that the foundation of a genuine morality lies in human nature itself. He showed what he took to be the failures of religion, but he also tried to show that man himself is responsible for the existence of society, and for its generally beneficial organization. Of course, his optimism was limited. He did not suppose mankind an entirely benevolent species. He did not suppose that a completely enlightened society was imminent, or even a long-range prospect. But he did see evidence of some generosity, of some virtuous motives, and of some significant rationality. It was on this foundation in human nature that he thought man had built. "Tho' justice be artificial," he wrote, "the sense of its morality is natural." To those who might think he was offering a merely relativistic account of these artificial virtues he went on to say:

> Most of the inventions of men are subject to change. They depend upon humour and caprice. They have a vogue for a time, and then sink into oblivion. It may, perhaps, be apprehended, that if justice were allow'd to be a human invention, it must be plac'd on the same footing. But the cases are widely different. The interest, on which justice is founded, is the greatest imaginable, and extends to all times and places. It cannot possibly be serv'd by any other invention. It is obvious, and discovers itself on the very first formation of society. All these causes render the rules of justice stedfast and immutable; at least, as immutable as human nature. (T 619-20)

Hume saw, correctly, I suggest, that morality is autonomous. It is, or at least it ought to be, free from the putative authority of religion and religious belief. He also thought it genuine, its distinctions in an important sense real, founded on the nature of mankind and the world in which we live.

Notes

In preparing this paper I have benefited from the use of "Bayle, Barbeyrac, and Hume," an unpublished paper by Prof. James Moore, and also from the comments of Profs. James Tully, Knud Haakonssen, Marcus Hester and J. B. Schneewind.

1. Abbreviations of works cited in the text are as follows:

> B: *Miscellaneous Reflections, Occasion'd by the Comet which appear'd in December 1680. Chiefly tending to explode Popular Superstitions*, Pierre Bayle, trans. from the French, 2 vols. (London: J. Morphew, 1708)

D: *Dialogues concerning Natural Religion*, David Hume, ed. N. Kemp Smith (Indianapolis: Bobbs-Merrill, 1947)

ECHU: Hume's *Enquiries concerning Human Understanding and*
ECPM: *concerning the Principles of Morals*, ed. L. A. Selby-Bigge and P. H. Nidditch, 3d ed. (Oxford: The Clarendon Press, 1975)

NHR: *Natural History of Religion*, in *David Hume: The Philosophical Works*, ed. T. H. Green and T. H. Grose, 4 vols. (Darmstadt: Scientia Verlag Aalen, 1964, reprint of edition of 1886)

P: *Of the Law of Nature and Nations*, Samuel Pufendorf, trans. by Basil Kennet, et al. with the notes by Jean Barbeyrac (London: J. Walthoe, et al., 1729)

T: *A Treatise of Human Nature*, David Hume, ed. L. A. Selby-Bigge and P. H. Nidditch, 2d ed. (Oxford: The Clarendon Press, 1978)

W: *David Hume: The Philosophical Works* cited above

2. *The Philosophical Works of Descartes*, ed. and trans. E. S. Haldane and G. R. T. Ross, 2 vols. (New York: Dover, 1955), 2:39.

3. For Bacon's views see his essays, "Of Atheism" and "Of Superstition." The remark by Grotius is from his *De jure belli ac pacis*, Prolegomena, as cited by Pufendorf, p. 142.

4. Richard Bentley, *The Folly of Atheism . . . A Sermon Preached in the Church of St. Martin in the Fields . . .* (London: Tho. Parkhurst, et al., 1692), p. 3, as reprinted in *Eight Boyle Lectures on Atheism 1692* (New York: Garland Publishing, 1976).

5. Bentley, p. 35. At this point Bentley has Hobbes particularly in mind.

6. John Locke, *The Second Treatise of Civil Government* and *A Letter Concerning Toleration*, ed. J. W. Gough (Oxford: Basil Blackwell, 1948), p. 156.

7. John Locke, *An Essay concerning Human Understanding*, ed. P. H. Nidditch (Oxford: The Clarendon Press, 1979), p. 74 (1.3.12).

8. MS. C28. fol. 141, cited from John Colman, *John Locke's Moral Philosophy* (Edinburgh: Edinburgh University Press, 1983), p. 46. Colman says: "The theory which is sketched in the *Two Tracts* and expounded in detail in the *Essays* is essentially theological and legalist. Locke holds that, were there no God or had He not promulgated a law to mankind there would be no such things as moral right and wrong, virtue and vice. He also maintains that...the ultimate reason a person has for living virtuously is that God's law is backed by sanctions, that in the next life virtue will be rewarded and vice punished." (p. 5)

9. Pufendorf (1632-1694) held the first chair of natural and international law at a German university (Heidelberg), was later Professor of Natural Law at Lund, Court Historian to, first, the King of Sweden, and then to the Elector of Brandenburg. Thirty years after Pufendorf's death, Francis Hutcheson said that he had become "the grand Instructor in Morals to all who have of late given themselves to that Study," while the Professor of Moral Philosophy at Edinburgh in the 1730s was, according to Alexander Carlyle, still basing his lectures on a short version of Pufendorf's *Of the Law of Nature and Nations*. See Hutcheson, *A Collection of Letters and Essays on Several Subjects, lately Publish'd in the Dublin Journal,* (London: J. Darby, et al., 1729), as reprinted in Francis Hutcheson, *Opera Minora* (Georg Olms: Hildesheim, 1971), pp. 102-03; and Carlyle, *Anecdotes and Characters of the Times,* ed. James Kinsley (London: Oxford University Press, 1973), p. 26. For a stimulating introduction to Pufendorf's ethical views and a brief account of recent work on him, see J. B. Schneewind, "Pufendorf and the History of Ethics," *Synthese,* forthcoming.

10. Although Hobbes was often thought to be an atheist, and was denounced soundly for his views, the explicit teaching of his *Leviathan* is close to that of Bentley, Pufendorf, and the other anti-atheists. He "only is properly said to reign," he writes, "that governs his subjects by his word, and by promise of rewards to those that obey it, and by threatening them with punishment that obey it not. Subjects therefore in the kingdom of God, are not bodies inanimate, nor creatures irrational; because they understand no precepts as his: nor atheists; nor they that believe not that God has any care of the actions of mankind; because they acknowledge no word for his, nor have hope of his rewards or fear of his threatenings. They therefore that believe there is a God that governeth the world, and hath given precepts, and propounded rewards, and punishments to mankind, are God's subjects; all the rest, are to be understood as enemies." (Part II.31, Oakeshott edition)

11. It was even doubted that there were any atheists on the grounds that no person who claimed to be an atheist could be trusted actually to be one, and especially since belief in God was thought unavoidable, it was clear the atheist was not telling the truth. As late as 1771 it was said that, while "Many people, both ancient and modern, have pretended to atheism . . . it is justly questioned whether any man seriously adopted such a principle. These pretensions, therefore, must be founded on pride or affectation." See "Atheist", in *Encyclopaedia Britannica; or, a Dictionary of Arts and Sciences, Compiled upon*

a New Plan, 3 vols. (Edinburgh: Bell and Macfarquhar, 1771), 1:501. For a helpful account of some seventeenth- and eighteenth-century attitudes toward atheism see David Berman, "The Genesis of Avowed Atheisim in Britain," *Question,* 11 (1978), 44-45, and "The Repressive Denials of Atheism in Britain in the Seventeenth and Eighteenth Centuries," *Proceedings of the Royal Irish Academy* 82 (1982), 211-45.

12. On Bayle in general see Elisabeth Labrousee, *Pierre Bayle. Tome 1, du pays de foix à la cité d'Erasme,* and *Pierre Bayle. Tome 2, Heterodoxie et rigorisme* (The Hague: Martinus Nijhoff, 1963, 1964). On Bayle and the atheist controversy, see Walter E. Rex, *Essays on Pierre Bayle and Religious Controversy* (The Hague: Martinus Nijhoff, 1965), pp. 30-74, and especially 33-35, 51. J.-P. Pittion, "Hume's Reading of Bayle: An Inquiry into the Source and Role of [Hume's] Memoranda," *Journal of the History of Philosophy,* XV (1977), 373-86, is also of interest here.

13. "Explanation I," *The Dictionary Historical and Critical of Mr. Peter Bayle,* trans. by P. Des Maizeaux, et al. 5 vols., 2d English edition (London: D. Midwinter, et al., 1734-1738), 5:811-14, especially 813. A convenient modern translation which includes this material is *Historical and Critical Dictionary,* ed. and trans. by R. H. Popkin (Indianapolis: Bobbs-Merrill, 1965).

14. *Miscellaneous Reflections* was first published as *Pensées diverses écrites à un Docteur de Sorbonne;* Bayle later published a *Continuation des Pensées diverses.*

15. On these uses of *atheist* and *atheism* see D. C. Allen, *Doubt's Boundless Sea* (Baltimore: Johns Hopkins University Press, 1964). Stanley's use of the term comes from his account of Pyrrhonism and is cited here from the entry for *atheist* in the *OED.*

16. Bentley's first Boyle Lecture (see above, n. 4) characterizes atheism as including "all the various Forms of Impiety; whether of such as excludes the Deity from governing the World by his Providence, or judging it by his Righteousness, or creating it by his Wisdom and Power . . . [and those] that not only disbelieve the *Christian* Religion; but impugn the assertion of a *Providence,* of the *Immortality* of the Soul, of an Universal *Judgment* to come, and of any *Incorporeal* Essence." All these views terminate, he says, "in downright Atheism. For the Divine Inspection into the affairs of the World doth necessarily follow from the Nature and Being of God. And he that denies this, doth implicitly deny his Existence . . . the Existence of God and his Government of the World do mutally suppose and imply one another." (pp. 5-6) The Boyle Lecturer of 1697, Francis Gastrell, gives much the same analysis: The atheist is one who "says there is no God that governs the world, and judgeth the earth; there is no God

that has appointed laws and rules for men to act by; there is no God to whom men are accountable for their actions." *The Certainty and Necessity of Religion in general* . . . (London, 1697). Cited from John Redwood, *Reason, Ridicule and Religion: The Age of Enlightenment in England, 1660-1750,* (Cambridge, Mass.: Harvard University Press, 1976), p. 30. Redwood's work is a useful compendium of materials on the atheist controversy.

17. Among those who appear to believe that Hume's religious position was correctly assessed by his contemporaries are David Berman and John Gaskin. See Berman's "David Hume and the Suppression of 'Atheism,'" *Journal of the History of Philosophy* 21 (1983), 375-87; and Gaskin's *Hume's Philosophy of Religion,* (London: Macmillan, 1978). Professor Gaskin's study is the most complete account of Hume's philosophy of religion, and one to which I am indebted. I have also learned from his "Hume, Atheism, and the 'Interested Obligation' of Morality," in *McGill Hume Studies,* ed. D. F. Norton, N. Capaldi, and W. Robison (San Diego: Austin Hill Press, 1978), 147-60.

18. See Hume's *Enquiry concerning Human Understanding,* Sections X and XI, and his *Dialogues concerning Natural Religion, passim.*

19. NHR 3:309-63. This work is discussed below.

20. Hume does grant that the belief in a deity cannot be eradicated entirely from the human race, and not even from most individuals. But given his views about the corrigibility of human belief, even of those beliefs that are universal, no interesting theological conclusions can be drawn from this fact. I have discussed Hume's views on belief in some detail in chapters 5 and 6 of *David Hume: Common Sense Moralist, Sceptical Metaphysician,* (Princeton: Princeton University Press, 1982). Hereafter cited as *David Hume.*

21. "Of the Immortality of the Soul," W 4:405-06.

22. For Boswell's account of his July 7, 1776 interview with Hume, see D 76-80.

23. It has often been noted that Hume reported to Henry Home (later Lord Kames) that he was "castrating" the *Treatise* of its nobler parts, or those dealing with religious issues, and likely to offend. Not so often noticed are his remarks to Francis Hutcheson, two years later, indicating that Book III of the *Treatise* was subjected to a similar round of revisions so as not to give offense to the religious. See *The Letters of David Hume,* ed J. Y. T. Greig, 2 vols. (Oxford: The Clarendon Press, 1932), I, 34, 36 (letters 13 and 15). Had not Hume so carefully altered the *Treatise,* it too, it seems safe to say, would be more explicitly critical of religious beliefs and practices.

24. For an account of these events and the changes made in the *Natural History,* see T. H. Grose, "History of the Editions," W 3:60-64, and

E. C. Mossner, *The Life of David Hume,* Edinburgh: Thomas Nelson, 1954), pp. 319-327, 619. Warburton's further views of NHR were published in *Remarks on Mr. David Hume's Essay on the Natural History of Religion,* London, 1757), a work he wrote in collaboration with Richard Hurd.

25. "They suppose their deities, however potent and invisible, to be nothing but a species of human creatures, perhaps raised from among mankind, and retaining all human passions and appetites, together with corporeal limbs and organs. Such limited beings, though masters of human fate, being, each of them, incapable of extending his influence every where, must be vastly multiplied, in order to answer that variety of events, which happen over the whole face of nature. Thus every place is stored with a crowd of local deities; and thus polytheism has prevailed, and still prevails, among the greatest part of uninstructed mankind. . . . every disastrous accident alarms us, and sets us on enquiries concerning the principles whence it arose: Apprehensions spring up with regard to futurity: And the mind, sunk into diffidence, terror, and melancholy, has recourse to every method of appeasing those secret intelligent powers, on whom our future is supposed entirely to depend." (NHR III; W 4:318-19)

26. "The intolerance of almost all religions, which have maintained the unity of God, is as remarkable as the contrary principle of the polytheists. . . . I may venture to affirm, that few corruptions of idolatry and polytheism are more pernicious to society than this corruption of theism, when carried to the utmost height." (NHR IX; W 4:337-38)

27. "To oppose the torrent of scholastic religion by such feeble maxims as these, that *it is impossible for the same thing to be and not to be,* that *the whole is greater than a part,* that *two and three make five;* is pretending to stop the ocean with a bull-rush. Will you set up profane reason against sacred mystery? No punishment is great enough for your impiety. And the same fires, which were kindled for heretics, will also serve for the destruction of philosophers." (NHR XI; W 4:342)

28. Hume closes Section IV by remarking: "It is great complaisance, indeed, if we dignify with the name of religion such an imperfect system of theology, and put it on a level with later systems, which are founded on principles more just and more sublime. For my part, I can scarcely allow the principles even of Marcus Aurelius, Plutarch, and some other *Stoics* and *Academics,* though much more refined than the pagan superstition, to be worthy of the honourable appellation of theism. For if the mythology of the heathens resemble the ancient European system of spiritual beings, excluding God and angels, and leaving only fairies and sprights; the creed of these philosophers may

justly be said to exclude a deity, and to leave only angels and fairies." (NHR IV; W 4:325)

29. Monotheism leads necessarily to greater corruption just because it achieves the higher and purer theory. While the supposed extent of the deity's "science and authority" increases, so do our "terrors naturally augment"; the "higher the deity is exalted in power and knowledge, the lower of course is he depressed in goodness and belevolence; whatever epithets of praise may be bestowed on him by his amazed adorers." It is this conflict, Hume goes on to suggest, which is responsible for the unhealthy mental state of many theists: their opinion itself, he says, "contracts a kind of falsehood, and belies the inward sentiment. The heart secretly destests such measures of cruel and implacable vengeance; but the judgment dares not but pronounce them perfect and adorable. And the additional misery of this inward struggle aggravates all the other terrors, by which these unhappy victims to superstition are for ever haunted." (NHR XII; W 4:354-55)

30. Bayle had found it necessary to grant that his argument in support of atheists was hypothetical only, for there was no known society of atheists to hold up as evidence. Hume, by identifying polytheism with atheism, avoids this problem and strengthens the atheistic position.

31. T 574; see also p. 618, where Hume speaks of his "system of ethics."

32. The theory I am discussing is perhaps more commonly called *voluntarism,* but, because some versions of voluntarism may not contain precisely the elements found in Pufendorf, Barbeyrac, etc., I have retained the more idiosyncratic term, *divine command theory.* Several of the presuppositions mentioned are espoused explicitly by Barbeyrac in his notes to Book II, chap. IV of Pufendorf's *Of the Law of Nature and Nations,* where the latter's popular *Abridgment of the Duties of a Man and Citizen,* giving "us a System of natural Religion; *i.e.* the Duties of Man to God," is summarized. See pp. 155ff. Note also Locke's remark in MS. C28, cited in note 8.

33. It has been suggested to me that this puts the matter too strongly, for to say that every activity of the deity is necessarily virtuous is to suggest a limitation on his activity not in accord with the views of the voluntarists. It appears, however, that the deity of even the most radical voluntarist is necessarily virtuous in every action, for, according to the voluntarist, the actions or commands of the deity define virtue: actions are good or right because the deity orders them or performs them.

34. A further such presupposition which Hume can be seen to oppose is

the view that understanding the law of the superior being on which one is dependent imposes on one the obligation to obey that law (in virtue, apparently, of the allegiance owed the superior being). Hume's objections to attempts to found morality on understanding alone are well known, and hence I shall here omit any discussion of his reasons for rejecting this particular presupposition, but my views on the subject are set out in chapter 3 of my *David Hume.*

35. By popular religion Hume simply means a religion of the people, in contrast to one limited to only a few philosophers.

36. For a brief account of Shaftesbury's objections to Locke and other Christian moralists, see *David Hume,* pp. 33-43. For Hutcheson's views of Pufendorf, see the remarks referred to above, note 8; for a discussion of his objections to Locke's ethics, see my "Hutcheson's Moral Realism," *Journal of the History of Philosophy,* 22 (July, 1985), 397-418. Bayle appears to have influenced both Shaftesbury (with whom he was personally well acquainted) and Hutcheson on the matter of the morality of atheists, while Hume, as is well known, acknowledges the influence of these two British moralists. Hume goes further than either Shaftesbury or Hutcheson, however, who are generally content to argue that atheists could be morally upright. See Shaftesbury's *An Inquiry concerning Virtue, or Merit,* Book I, Part III, and Hutcheson's *Illustrations upon the Moral Sense,* Section VI, v-vii.

37. Boswell reports of Hume (on his death bed): "He then said flatly that the Morality of every Religion was bad, and, I really thought, was not jocular when he said, 'that when he heard a man was religious, he concluded he was a rascal, though he had known some instances of very good men being religious.'" Boswell then adds, significantly: "This was just an extravagant reverse of the common remark as to Infidels." (D 76)

38. Hobbes and Locke, Hume writes "maintained the selfish system of morals." He then adds: "The most obvious objection to the selfish hypothesis is, that, as it is contrary to common feeling and our most unprejudiced notions, there is required the highest stretch of philosophy to establish so extraordinary a paradox. To the most careless observer there appear to be such dispositions as benevolence and generosity; such affections as love, friendship, compassion, gratitude. These sentiments have their causes, effects, objects, and operations, marked by common language and observation, and plainly distinguished from those of the selfish passions. . . . I shall not here enter into any detail on the present subject. Many able philosophers have shown the insufficiency of these systems. And I shall take for granted what, I believe, the smallest reflection will make evident to every impartial enquirer." (ECPM 296, 298) For a somewhat more detailed

discussion of Hume's views on the egoism of these writers see *David Hume*, pp. 43–48.

39. Hume says that "there are certain calm desires and tendencies, which, tho' they be real passions, produce little emotion in the mind . . . These desires are of two kinds; either certain instincts originally implanted in our natures, such as benevolence and resentment . . . or the general appetite to good, and aversion to evil, consider'd merely as such . . . The common error of metaphysicians has lain in ascribing the direction of the will entirely to one of these principles, and supposing the other to have no influence. Men often act knowingly against their interest." (T 417–18)

There is an element of ambiguity in the concept of fear found in much Christian teaching, such that fear as awe or respect is fundamental to the ethics of this teaching ("The fear of the Lord is the beginning of wisdom"), while fear in the more ordinary sense is the motivational complement of self-interested hope, or hope of reward. The anti-atheists seem to trade on this ambiguity; Hume seems perfectly willing to let them do so, and to take rhetorical advantage of this fact by treating the two forms of fear as one.

40. Hume continues: "To suppose, that the mere regard to the virtue of the action, may be the first motive, which produc'd the action, and render'd it virtuous, is to reason in a circle. Before we can have such a regard, the action must be really virtuous; and this virtue must be deriv'd from some virtuous motive: And consequently the virtuous motive must be different from the regard to the virtue of the action . . . . Here is a man, that does many belevolent actions. . . . No character can be more amiable and virtuous. We regard these actions as proofs of the greatest humanity. *This humanity bestows a merit on the actions.* A regard to this merit is, therefore, a secondary consideration, and deriv'd from the antecedent principle of humanity, which is meritorious and laudable." (Emphasis added.)

James Tully has pointed out to me that some of those Hume is opposing would likely respond by claiming that, although religious belief or practice may begin in self-interest (fear for his or her eternal state leads the reprobate to act in accordance with the precepts of Christianity), it can go beyond that to the point that the saint loses all concern for self. This is an important claim, and one that Hume would have to take seriously, for his own account of the development of the artificial virtues could be seen as a secularized version of a similar transition: a concern for my property can lead me to an overriding concern for justice, or the good of society. Hume's response, I speculate, would take the form of a reminder: the action of the saint may indeed be selfless, but this does not prove that such virtue originates in the fear of eternal punishment or the hope of eternal reward. On the contrary, it has its origin in a restricted and restrictive concern, that which gives rise to the artificial virtues. For an outline of the line of a further defense Pufendorf might have taken in response to criticisms of his divine command theory, see the final section of the article by J. B. Schneewind cited in note 9.

41. The context in which this remark is made bears repeating here: "The duties, which a man performs as a friend or parent, seem merely owing to his benefactor or children; nor can he be wanting to these duties, without breaking through all the ties of nature and morality. A strong inclination may prompt him to the performance: A sentiment of order or moral obligation joins its force to these natural ties: And the whole man, if truly virtuous, is drawn to his duty, without any effort or endeavour. Even with regard to the virtues, which are more austere, and more founded on reflection, such as public spirit, filial duty, temperance, or integrity; the moral obligation, in our apprehension, removes all pretension to religious merit; and the virtuous conduct is deemed no more than what we owe to society and to ourselves." (NHR XIV; W 4:358-59)

42. *Letters of David Hume,* I, 40. Hume's argument in the *Treatise* is generally supposed to be directed against the rationalists. He there mentions only Wollaston, but the second *Enquiry* indicates that he also had Malebranche, Cudworth, and Clarke in mind. (ECPM 197) The argument bears equally against other ethical theories dependent upon claims that neither have been nor can be confirmed by experience. If it is argued that the divine command theory is the contrary of that of Cudworth and the other rationalists—that it is voluntaristic and based on a revelation that does or may run contrary to reason—then one need only to turn to "Of Miracles" to determine Hume's response to an ethics that in this alternative manner takes us beyond, perhaps further beyond, our experience.

43. Hume says that the "ideas" of *property, right,* and *obligation* "are altogether unintelligible without first understanding" the idea of justice, one of the most important virtues. He then adds: "Those, therefore, who make use of the word *property,* or *right,* or *obligation,* before they have explained the origin of justice, or even make use of [these words] in that explication, are guilty of a very gross fallacy, and can never reason upon any solid foundation. . . . 'Tis very preposterous, therefore, to imagine that we can have any idea of property, without fully comprehending the nature of justice, and shewing its origin in the artifice and contrivance of men." (T 490-91) This remark should be compared to that of Barbeyrac, found above, p. 109.

44. This distinction between the natural and the artificial virtues is found

in several places in Hume's writings. In his essay "Of the Original Contract" it is put very succinctly: "All *moral* duties may be divided into two kinds. The *first* are those, to which men are impelled by a natural instinct or immediate propensity, which operates on them, independent of all ideas of obligation, and of all views, either to public or private utility. Of this nature are, love of children, gratitude to benefactors, pity to the unfortunate. When we reflect on the advantage, which results to society from such humane instincts, we pay them the just tribute of moral approbation and esteem: But the person, actuated by them, feels their power and influence, antecedent to any such reflection.

"The *second* kind of moral duties are such as are not supported by any original instinct of nature, but are performed entirely from a sense of obligation, when we consider the necessities of human society, and the impossibility of supporting it, if these duties were neglected. It is thus *justice* or a regard to the property of others, *fidelity* or the observance of promises, become obligatory, and acquire an authority over mankind." (W 3:454–55)

45. Although one wishes that Hume had said more about the transformation of self-interest into virtue, he is at least clear that the artificial virtues arise in the manner outlined here: "Afterwards a sentiment of morals concurs with interest, and becomes a new obligation upon mankind." (T 523)

46. Hume's account of the origin of government and allegiance first appeared in the *Treatise*, 3.2.7–10. A shorter version was published as "Of the Origin of Government," in the 1777 edition of the *Essays and Treatises*, and is found at W 4:113–17. The fact that the essay was one of the last of the works for which Hume arranged publication suggests that he attached great importance to the subject, and also reveals the continuity of his thought on this matter. In both the *Treatise* and the posthumous essay he traces the origin of government to the need to overcome our tendency to overlook our real or distant interests in favour of apparent or present attractions, and both present allegiance as a "factitious duty of obedience" or submission to the magistrate, but this phrase is from the essay of 1777. In the *Treatise* Hume says that "all government is plainly an invention of men." Consequently, allegiance, on his view, is also a human invention. (T 542)

47. The anti-atheists may seem to have a ready and valid objection to Hume's account of obligation: it is not in fact an account of *obligation*, but merely one possible description of the manner in which the *sense of duty* arises. And even those who do not share the religious commitments of the anti-atheists may feel that Hume, in an effort to demystify morality by stripping it of its transcendental elements, has

not so much explained obligation as he has explained it away, into a (mere) *sense* of duty: *obligation* entails an *obliger*, separate from the individual *obliged*, it may be thought. But, bearing in mind that Hume insists that this sense of duty has a genuine foundation in human nature, his explanation seems entirely consistent with his general philosophical program. It appears to be an analogue, for example, of his explanation of the idea of necessary connection. And the feeling that obligation, to be genuine, necessarily entails more than mere inner compulsion, may be a mere vestige of transcendentally based morality. But even if there is a satisfactory Humean response to this objection, it does appear that Hume's account of obligation is underdeveloped. Knud Haakonssen has pointed this out and gone on to suggest how on Hume's view we develop obligations to justice, fidelity, allegiance, and the remaining artificial virtues. See "Hume's Obligations," *Hume Studies* 4 (1978), 7-17, reprinted in Haakonssen's valuable *The Science of a Legislator: The Natural Jurisprudence of David Hume & Adam Smith* (Cambridge: Cambridge University Press, 1981), pp. 30-35.